WHAT JAZZ IS ALL ABOUT

WHAT JAZZ IS
ALL ABOUT

by LILLIAN ERLICH

*Illustrated with a portrait
gallery of jazz greats*

JULIAN MESSNER, INC.
New York

Published by Julian Messner, Inc.
8 West 40th Street, New York 18

Published simultaneously in Canada
by The Copp Clark Publishing Co. Limited

Second Printing, 1963

Photographs used with the permission of the following: Associated Booking Corp., Atlantic Records, Blue Note Records, Charlie Parker Record Corp., Columbia Records, Folkway Records, Jazz Arts Society, MGM/Verve Records, Monte Kay Management, Music Corporation of America, RCA Victor Records, Riverside Records, Roulette Records, Shaw Artists Corporation, Tempo Music, Inc., Mrs. Lester Young

Printed in the United States of America
Library of Congress Catalog Card No. 62-16677

For my husband, John

CONTENTS

A Portrait Gallery of Jazz Greats

Leadbelly

Big Bill Broonzy

2

Bessie Smith

3

Louis Armstrong

4

Count Basie

Jimmy Rushing

Duke Ellington

Duke Ellington and Orchestra

Fats Waller

Billie Holiday

Mahalia Jackson

Bix Beiderbecke

Gene Krupa

Earl "Fatha" Hines

Fletcher Henderson

Jack Teagarden

Coleman Hawkins

13

Benny Goodman

Ella Fitzgerald

Paul Desmond

Teddy Wilson

Thelonious Monk

Charlie Parker

Dizzy Gillespie

Gerry Mulligan

Stan Kenton

Woody Herman

21

Lester Young

Miles Davis

Dave Brubeck

Jimmy Giuffre

Ray Charles

2 5

Art Blakey

Julian "Cannonball" Adderley

Sonny Rollins

Charlie Mingus

Ornette Coleman

Miles Davis and Gil Evans

Gil Evans

Modern Jazz Quartet

John Lewis

George Russell

THE DEEP ROOTS

African Drums and European Folk Tunes

Jazz was born and bred in America. It grew slowly through a complicated blending of African rhythms and European musical ideas—in the way that could have happened only on American soil by the most fortunate coming together of people, time and place. The miracle is that jazz happened at all —and is still happening—a new and unique art form that keeps growing and changing in our own time.

The broad base of jazz is Negro folk music created in slave days. This is the music of southern fields and slave quarters and country churches, music that for two and a half centuries expressed the deepest feelings of the Negro people. Into this music they poured the rhythms of Africa, remembered and handed down from generation to generation; with these rhythms they transformed the ballads and hymns brought across the Atlantic Ocean by settlers from all over western Europe. This was the mixture that produced spirituals and blues, that brought voodoo drums and French band music together in New Orleans, and that still permeates jazz.

The first slave ship to reach America landed at Jamestown,

Virginia, in 1619. It carried a cargo of fourteen Negroes who were quickly sold to the highest bidders. There was a great demand for slaves as the colonies expanded; indeed, the whole agricultural economy of the South was built on slave labor. The slave trade flourished for over two centuries. The slave population grew enormously as new shipments of Africans reached the New World and as new generations were born into bondage. The United States government banned the slave traffic in 1808, but Negroes were smuggled into the country until Civil War days. When President Lincoln signed the Emancipation Proclamation, there were four million slaves to set free.

American slaves came from West Africa, from a vast coastal area that stretched from Senegal in the north to the Gulf of Guinea in the south. Slave dealers roamed this region, setting tribe against tribe so that they could barter for the captives. They treated the captured Africans like cattle, or worse. Men, women and children were packed tight and chained in the holds of sailing ships. Many of them died during the long voyage across the Atlantic.

Those who survived the passage in the slave ships found themselves in a harsh and bewildering world. They were separated from their tribes, forbidden to speak their own languages. They became the absolute property of their masters. They could be bought or sold at any time, even won or lost in a card game. Mothers were separated from children, husbands from wives. They could be worked as long or as hard as their masters wished and punished as their masters saw fit. They had no possessions, no freedom of movement, no recourse to law. Even with the kindest of masters, slaves lived narrowly restricted lives without hope for the future.

It seems remarkable that these Negroes were able to create a beautiful and compelling folk music under such conditions. But the truth may be that the institution of slavery, cruel as it was, helped rather than hindered the development of this music and gave it emotional depth.

For two and a half centuries, slaves were kept ignorant and isolated from the mainstream of American life. It was exactly this isolation that made them cling to their ancient musical traditions and find channels, in the midst of many prohibitions, through which they could express their deepest feelings. From the beginning, slaveowners, to prevent revolt, tried to stamp out African languages, drumming and religious rites. Nevertheless, the spirit of African music survived and was constantly refreshed by the arrival of new slaves from Africa. Their native rhythms went underground at times but never really disappeared. The African concept of music as a communal, creative activity was always there. It is at the heart of American Negro folk music—and of jazz.

Some people think that Negroes have a special inborn rhythmic sense. It seems more likely that the West Africans who were brought to America as slaves had simply developed through long practice a high degree of rhythmic skill. They came from a culture that happened to have highly complicated rhythms. Everybody—men, women and children—participated in music and dance. The slaves were conditioned to rhythms that were a part of their speech, their songs and their body movements.

One generation of Negroes handed these rhythms down to the next in the lullabies sung to babies, in the movements of women grinding corn, in the songs of men hoeing in the fields. Negro children at prayer meetings heard the foot-tapping and hand-clapping of their elders and passed the syncopated beat along to *their* children.

All music is based on rhythm, melody and harmony. In West African music, rhythm was by far the most important of these elements. The "beat" dominated every musical performance, and melody and harmony were weak by comparison. In Europe, music developed in the opposite direction. Rhythm stayed in the background, while melody and harmony became increasingly elaborate and important.

The ancestors of American slaves used music in everyday life to an extent unknown in the West. In Africa, music served many useful purposes. West Africans had no written language, so they used songs to preserve the history of each tribe and its laws and traditions. These songs kept alive the heroes of the past and the stories of ancient migrations and battles. They helped educate the young in the ways of the tribe.

Music marked every milestone of life from birth to death. Singing, drumming and dancing marked a boy's initiation into manhood, his marriage, his forays as a hunter or a warrior. The smallest event—even a child's loss of his first baby tooth —could have a special song. A major event, such as a funeral, required long and elaborate ceremonies, always with musical accompaniment. All these rituals were more or less religious in character. They welded tribes together and strengthened the authority of chieftains and priests.

West Africans sang as they worked, too. They usually worked in groups, and songs set the pace and made the work seem more like a game. In these songs as well as the religious ones, the singers used a call and response pattern. A leader made a statement in song, and then a chorus repeated the statement, added to it, or exclaimed about it.

In America, the work songs of southern Negroes fell naturally into the same leader-chorus form. So did religious songs and spirituals. As jazz evolved, it used this interplay of voices in many ways.

Unlike Europeans, who liked changes of mood in their music, West Africans used music to create a single mood. They used tireless repetition in singing, drumming and dancing. This repetition had a powerful, hypnotic effect. It spurred warriors to battle, or induced a trancelike state in religious ceremonies. Singers and dancers in religious rites seemed transported to another world. Sometimes they became "possessed." They lost contact with their surroundings and flung themselves about or fell to the ground.

The short musical phrase which was repeated over and over again in African ceremonies reminds us of the riff—a short musical phrase used in jazz. The jazz riff is a two-to-four-bar passage, usually strong in rhythm, that is meant to be repeated. It can be played over and over by a soloist or tossed back and forth between sections of a band.

When Africans sang, they slid into and around notes instead of hitting them straight. They didn't stay on pitch. Their voices played around it; and the slides and swoops gave their songs a strange haunting quality quite unlike anything known in Western music. American Negroes, in slave days, sang with the same changes of pitch and the same subtle gliding from note to note.

It seems likely that the blues sound—so important in jazz—goes back to the African way of singing between and around notes. In blues, the third and seventh notes of the scale are flatted—not by a half tone, to which we are accustomed, but by a fraction closer to a quarter tone.

These slurred notes occur all through Negro folk music and jazz. The great blues singer, Bessie Smith, could slide easily into tones that can't be placed exactly on the scale. So could Billie Holiday. Ella Fitzgerald and Mahalia Jackson, among present-day singers, swoop and glide into notes in a way impossible to put down on paper. This is the opposite of the European musical tradition. A classically trained singer is taught to hit notes in a straightforward, precise way. To such a singer a deviation from pitch is a catastrophe. This difference in training may explain why opera singers do not make good blues singers.

West Africans used vibrato in their songs, and this, too, was adopted in jazz. Vibrato is a slightly tremulous or pulsating effect. African singers used this device to make certain parts of their songs more important or to give them emotional intensity. In jazz, vibrato serves much the same purpose and also sets up a rhythmic pulsation within the larger rhythm of the piece—a beat within a beat.

The West Africans knew and used several different musical instruments. Besides simple rhythm makers like rattles and bone clappers, they had a stringed instrument that was the ancestor of the American banjo. They also used a marimba-like instrument made of gourds strung up and played with two sticks—the granddaddy of the vibraphone. But their most important instruments were drums, and these produced the fantastic rhythms that so shaped Negro music through the centuries.

West African drums were made of hollow logs with heads of animal skins. These drums were tuned; that is, the heads were stretched to different degrees of tightness by means of pegs driven into the wood. They were made to imitate the sounds of the human voice—male and female—and even words. They were in a real sense "speaking drums," through which the gods were thought to speak. The drummer both beat the drum and vibrated it with his knee or elbow to produce different effects. The drums could plead or speak gently; they could also threaten and growl.

Usually two to six drums were used—each drummer developing his own complicated beat. The rhythms were insistent, driving, hypnotically powerful. They were orderly—but not with any order to which we are accustomed. There was nothing like the four-beat measure of time, and there were no absolute rules about where accents had to fall. A West African drummer accented every fifteenth beat if he felt like it. Imagine the rhythmic complications when several drums sounded together, each one using a different downbeat.

Many recordings have been made of African drum music. "The Royal Drums of the Abatutsi" (Riverside LP 4002) is a good example. Although fairly recently made, this recording gives a good idea of traditional African drumming, which has changed very little through the centuries. Jazzmen listen to African drums with mixed feelings of admiration and frustration, for jazz has never been able to match these complex rhythms.

West African music is not in itself jazz. It should not be expected to sound like jazz. Modern jazz has been three and a half centuries in the making; and the African strain that arrived here with the first slave ships has been thoroughly mixed with many different kinds of music in our culture.

The white settlers who were in the colonies when slavery began, came from all levels of European society. Along with their guns, their clothing and provisions, they brought to the New World the music of their native lands. Ordinary people knew ballads, drinking songs and dance tunes. Educated upper class colonists knew about the beginnings of opera and symphonic music. And everyone knew hymns.

Music was truly "in the air" in colonial America. Books were scarce, and many people couldn't read anyhow. They had to entertain themselves, and they made the most of their musical talents.

The white settlers, like the West Africans, had musical roots that reached deep into the past. In ancient times, Europeans used rhythm in a free, unfettered way. But about 1150, composers began to write "measured" music. They marked off lines of musical notation into even bars—each one containing the same number of beats. This was considered a great musical advance, but it also proved something of a straitjacket to rhythm. With the invention of measured music, a steady unchanging beat became the rule.

When Negro slaves heard the monotonous rhythm of Western music, their instinctive reaction was to add extra beats and shift the accents to make a livelier sound. In this way they gave an African pulse to an endless number of white ballads and hymns.

Western melody started as simply as the songs of Africa— with human speech as the springboard. The folk songs of Europe used simple melodies clustered around a few notes, and the slaves felt at home with them. The colonists also brought to America weakened versions of English, Dutch and Italian madrigals. These were songs for several voices, which were popular in Europe all through the Middle Ages. The voices did not harmonize. Each singer had a separate melodic part that overlapped or wove in and out of the tunes sung by others. This was similar to the way West Africans sang together, overlapping calls and responses in a complicated way. Madrigals were especially popular with educated Englishmen, many of whom could read music at sight; and madrigal singing was a favorite pastime of plantation society in the old South.

In general, the slaves did not adopt a Western melody in its entirety. Instead they took one or two lines out of a piece of music and repeated them. They also changed the sound by attacking the notes in the African way—with slides and slurs and vibrato effects.

Rhythm and melody come naturally to men—even in cultures as different as those of Europe and West Africa. But harmony had to be invented, and it arrived rather late on the musical scene. The idea of sounding separate notes together to produce chords started, or at least was first noted, in Europe in the ninth century. By the time America was colonized,

European music contained highly developed and complex harmonies.

Harmony must have sounded strange indeed to the slaves. Not that harmony was entirely unknown in Africa. Whenever people sing together, some natural and accidental harmonies occur. But the sophisticated chordal system of Western music was quite different from any harmonizing to which the Africans were accustomed.

From the earliest times new songs sprang up on American soil. Poets wrote verses about the events of the day and fitted them to traditional tunes. These songs were printed on broadsides and sold in the streets. They were so popular that the New England preacher, Cotton Mather, thundered warnings against "foolish songs and ballads which hawkers and peddlers carry to all parts of the country."

In the South, English traditional tunes were kept very much alive. Many an old ballad brought to Virginia by early settlers moved into the southern mountains and was preserved there—Elizabethan diction and all. "Careless Love" was an English ballad handed down from generation to generation of mountain folk before it became a Negro blues.

All through the colonies, people sang and fiddled and danced. In New England, the upper classes danced minuets. The French aristocrats in Louisiana danced quadrilles—borrowed from French court life. Lower in the social scale, there were Scottish reels and Irish jigs.

Songs were drawn from many lands. The tune of "Yankee Doodle," the battle song of the Revolutionary War, has been traced to a Dutch harvest song. "Auld Lang Syne" came from Scotland, "The Last Rose of Summer" from Ireland, "Barbara Allen" from England. "Home Sweet Home" had American lyrics but the tune was English; "The Old Oaken Bucket" used American lyrics with a Scottish tune. That old standard, "For He's a Jolly Good Fellow" (otherwise known as "The

Bear Went Over the Mountain" or "We Won't Get Home Until Morning"), goes back to a French song of the Middle Ages.

In the second half of the eighteenth century America took several large steps forward musically. Native American composers began to publish original works. American audiences were introduced to concerts and operas. At the same time part singing and clavichord playing were in vogue.

On the popular level there were lively dance tunes, sea chanties, political jingles. All these went into the grab bag of American popular song.

How did this music reach the slaves? Plantation owners kept their slaves ignorant and isolated. A real, if invisible, wall separated these Negroes from the rest of American society; but there were many chinks in the wall, and it was impossible to plug them all. Slaves who worked as house servants heard songs their masters knew; they also heard the tunes played by fiddlers at parties and balls. Field hands heard snatches of Irish or Scottish airs whistled by their overseers. Negro children imitated the game songs of white children. Music also traveled to some extent from plantation to plantation. It was carried not only by white visitors but by slaves sold from owner to owner.

The Negroes eagerly reached out for all the music that came their way. They flocked to the "Big House" when parties were held, pressing forward in the dark to hear the music that floated through open windows.

Most plantation owners, interested in converting their slaves to Christianity, encouraged hymn singing. The Negroes sang hymns with fervor and infused the simple melodies with new beauty and sadness. Negro spirituals, which were created during the last years of slavery, are often considered the highest attainment of Negro folk music. Solidly based on hymns learned from white masters, these spirituals are nevertheless

African in their powerful rhythms; and their emotional intensity was forged in the experience of slavery.

White people were from the beginning stirred by Negro music just as Negroes were stirred by the ballads and hymns of the white culture. White children absorbed lullabies with African turns of melody from their Negro nurses; and their elders responded to the gaiety of the Negroes' play music, the earthy rhythms of their hollers and work songs, and the poetry and deep feeling of their spirituals.

The ferment that was to produce jazz was already at work in the music of slave days.

CHAPTER TWO

BORN IN SLAVERY

Field Hollers and Work Songs

A holler is speech on the way to becoming song. It's the sound of a cowboy shouting at his cattle, the yell of a lumberjack as a tree crashes to the ground, the cry of a junkman —"any rags, any bottles, today?"—on a city street. When a man hollers, he lets the words shape the tune and the rhythm. His cry wells up out of his thoughts and feelings of the moment.

Among American Negroes in slave days, the holler was the song of the lonely field hand. A slave hoeing in a hot dusty field, far from other workers, would raise his voice to holler out his loneliness, his weariness, his yearning for a better life. His cry was half yell, half song. It started with a high drawn-out shout or yodel and then glided down to the lowest note he could reach.

This was the deep song of the South, the "cry," the strange and stirring sound that was to transform American music. Of all the Negro music created in slave days, the holler was closest to African sources, the least touched by other music in the American environment. When a slave hollered, he used falsetto phrases, slid and swooped from note to note, and used unexpected changes of rhythm. He might borrow a scrap of melody from a white man's ballad or hymn, but the style of singing was all his own—rooted in the African past.

At the end of slavery, hollers moved with Negro laborers onto the docks and into the construction camps of the South. Wherever Negroes worked at lonely backbreaking jobs, they hollered their mournful songs. Dock workers loading heavy bales of cotton on a Mississippi riverboat sang:

> Oh-h-h-h
> Po' roustabout don't have no home,
> Makes his livin' on his shoulder bone. . . .

A railroad worker driving steel spikes to clinch track to ties poured all the loneliness and longing of his rootless life into his cry:

> O—Lu-La!
> O—La-awd, gal!
> I wanta see you so bad. . . .

Negro boatmen on the Mississippi used hollers, too. Their sounding calls, which told the depth of the river and helped the pilot keep clear of dangerous shoals, were like field hollers —fragments of melody that were half sung, half shouted. They used the same haunting notes and the same slides and swoops of the voice as other hollerers. The most famous of these cries, "mark twain!" referred to the sounding line—the twine or "twain" that was lowered into the swirling river water to test its depth. Samuel Clemens took his pen name, Mark Twain, from this cry. Harry Belafonte used it as the theme of one of his best known songs.

Many Negro hollers have been recorded for the Archive of Folk Song of the Library of Congress in Washington, a great storehouse of all the different kinds of music that make up America's musical heritage. (A number of the recordings in this collection are available to the public on LP or 78 rpm disks. They are sold only by the Library of Congress. A *Catalog of Folk Music* costs twenty-five cents and may be ordered from the Recording Laboratory, Music Division, Library of Congress, Washington, 25, D.C.)

Hollers at first hearing may seem crude and monotonous. But when we listen to them over and over, we marvel at the subtle shifts of pitch and at the inner complications of their rhythms. We hear untaught singers play with the beat—slow it down and hold it back in an artful way that presages the retarded beat of jazz. Above all, we are struck by the emotional power of this music. The sorrow and longing and rough joy of the hollers well up out of deep feelings that are common to all mankind.

American Negro work songs are close relatives of hollers. They are songs of group labor—as distinguished from the hollers of solitary toil. Work songs use holler-like tunes, but they are more powerfully rhythmical than hollers, and they are cast in a distinctive form of their own—a "call and response" pattern in which the song passes back and forth between a leader and chorus.

Work songs date back to the beginning of slavery and have their roots in the communal work customs of West Africa. They set the pace for Negro work gangs through three centuries of hard physical labor on American soil. The words of work songs tell the story of the building of the South—of land cleared and plowed and planted; of rivers dammed and levees raised; of roads built and railroad track laid.

American Negro work songs, like hollers, have all but disappeared in the wake of tractors and steam shovels. But such songs can still be found in primitive cultures that depend on communal hand labor. In Haiti, farmers still gather to till each other's fields to the accompaniment of bamboo flutes, drums and singing. In other unmechanized parts of the world, men row boats, raise houses and cut wood to the steady beat of work songs. These songs are timed to work motions. They keep the workers moving together at the same pace so that they don't get in each other's way or get diverted from the main task. At the same time they make hard work enjoyable —more like a game or a dance.

This was the work-singing tradition brought to the colonies from Africa with the first slave ships. It didn't take slave-owners long to realize that the Negroes were used to work-ing in gangs and that they could work harder and faster to song. The masters encouraged their slaves to sing for the same reason that modern factory owners pipe music to their work-ers—to speed up production. From the beginning, song lead-ers got favored treatment. Men who could keep their com-panions moving at a good clip were given lighter tasks during slave days. After the Civil War, they were paid more in con-struction camps and were given special privileges in southern prisons.

The early work songs of southern Negroes were almost purely African in sound and form. They were little more than hollers—scraps of melody that slid from falsetto notes to deep grunts—repeated over and over by the song leader with the rest of the men chiming in with a word or line of response. As time went on, these songs merged with ballads and re-ligious songs of the outside world and moved closer to what was to become the blues.

Among the earliest work songs were rowing songs, sung as slaves pulled on the oars of flat-bottom boats on the rivers of the South. These songs were almost exactly like African ones, with two measures of song for each full stroke of the oars and with a song leader setting the pace and making up the words which his companions would repeat in unison.

The words of rowing songs were often religious, for boats

symbolized to the slaves a means of escape from earthly burdens. In these songs, any river was the River Jordan; and hosts of angels waited to welcome the weary oarsmen on the far shore.

> Michael row de boat ashore, Hallelujah!
> Michael boat a gospel boat, Hallelujah!

These haunting songs, with their strong rhythms, their call and response form, and their blending of sadness and religious exaltation, survived in Negro spirituals. "Swing Low, Sweet Chariot," "One More River to Cross" and "River Jordan" have the tempo of the old rowing songs and use the same images to promise a better life in the next world.

Negro rowing songs also had a great influence on sea chanties. It's strange but true that songs born on American rivers and sung by slaves spread to all the oceans of the world. The flat-bottomed cotton boats of the eighteenth century were run almost entirely by Negroes. When double-stacked wooden steamboats became the queens of the rivers in the nineteenth century, Negro stevedores worked on their freight decks. On the levees, Negroes loaded and unloaded hogsheads of tobacco and molasses, bales of cotton and crates of dry goods. Their songs sprang from the rowing songs of earlier generations of slaves; but the motions of lifting and carrying cargo, the burst of relief as each heavy load was thrust down, gave the songs a new tempo:

> I'm gwine to Alabamy—*Oh!*
> For to see my mammy—*Ah!*
> She went from old Virginny—*Oh!*
> And I'm her pickaninny—*Ah!*

Songs like this were picked up by white sailors and stevedores who worked on the same ships and docks as Negro

slaves. Many white sailors, English and Irish, worked season-
ally in southern cotton ports—especially Mobile and New
Orleans—in the peaceful decades between the War of 1812
and the Civil War. Many clipper ships of the same period
carried both white and Negro crewmen. Inevitably, white sea
chanties and Negro work songs got scrambled together—with
lasting effect on chanty singing around the world. "Shallo
Brown" and "Gimme de Banjo" are widely traveled seafar-
ing songs with American Negro antecedents.

Work songs of all kinds survived the end of slavery as
Negroes became the hired manual laborers of the South. The
Negroes were untrained, except in the most menial plantation work, and were ignorant of life in the outside world.
Some stayed on the farms, but many others drifted into construction camps, where they built levees, dug roads, and laid
railroad track. They were paid little, sometimes cheated, were
often in trouble with the law. The work songs of this period
took on new meanings. They reflect the loneliness of men
wandering from job to job, and their frightened and bitter
preoccupation with sheriffs and prison.

Work songs about railroad construction in the South tell
a dramatic story. Negro section hands, called "gandy dancers," did the backbreaking labor that covered the South with
a maze of steel track. Each section of track weighed almost
two tons and was handled by twelve or fourteen men. The
song leader had to keep these men moving together in a
smooth dancelike rhythm to distribute the strain evenly as
they unloaded track from flat cars. He called out directions
in a rhythmic chant:

> Be careful now, boys,
> Don't get hurt,
> I want you to go home,
> Lookin' all right.

There were special songs for clinching the track to the ties. The workers whirled their hammers in unison as they drove in the steel spikes:

> Dis ole hammer—*huh!*
> Kilt John Henry—*huh!*
> Can't kill me—*huh!*
> Can't kill me—*huh!*

Track lining meant straightening the steel track—one of the hardest of the jobs done by the railroad crews. The men lined up on each side of the track with their crowbars jammed under the rail. As the caller sang out directions, they heaved these bars. The rhythm of track lining set up a natural syncopation:

> Sis Joe, on the M 'n O,
> Track heavy, but she will go.

These were the raw materials of jazz. The rhythmic bending and lifting and heaving of the gandy dancers, the songs of the caller, the rattle and clank of the railroad cars, the lonesome sound of the train whistle—all merged into jazz and left an indelible mark on it.

America's best-known folk ballad, "John Henry," started as a song of Negro railroad builders and grew and changed through the years as it passed back and forth between Negro and white singers.

"John Henry" celebrates a Negro folk hero, a mighty steel driver who challenged a steam drill to a race and won. The version we know has strong traces of Scottish melody; and some of the words come straight out of English ballads. Part of one verse goes, "Oh, who's gonna shoe your pretty little foot, who's gonna glove your little hand?" The original can be found in the *Oxford Book of English Verse*.

One theory holds that John Henry was a real man who worked on the construction of the Big Bend tunnel for the Cincinnati and Ohio Railroad in 1873. The tunnel ran through a rocky mountain in a wild part of West Virginia, and working in it was grueling and dangerous. Besides the suffocating heat inside the tunnel, the choking dust and smoke of blasting, there was the constant menace of falling rock and cave-ins. Most of the workers were Negroes. Many lost their lives before the tunnel was finished.

John Henry, the story goes, was a Negro steel driver, a giant of legendary strength, who could swing his hammer all day long driving a steel spike into solid rock to make holes for blasting charges. When a white boss tried to introduce a steam drill, John Henry offered to match himself against the machine.

> John Henry told his cap'n,
> Said "A man ain't nothin' but a man;
> And before I'd let that steam drill beat me down,
> I'd die with a hammer in my hand,
> Lawd, lawd, I'd die with a hammer in my hand."

In the legend, John Henry won the contest but lost his life:

> He drove so hard he broke his pore heart
> An' he lied down his hammer and died. . . .

Whether he actually died of his exertions or was crushed to death in a later landslide, as some folklorists claim, John Henry had proved that man is superior to his tools.

The heroes of American Negro folk songs are often animals. Like Br'er Rabbit in the Uncle Remus stories, these animals stand for the Negro himself. They are small and seemingly weak; but they outwit and outlast their strongest enemies. The Grey Goose and the Boll Weevil are two such animal heroes.

"The Grey Goose" is one of the most famous of all Negro ballad-work songs. It celebrates a wild goose who was shot, plucked, cooked, carved, and run through a sawmill—and then flew away at the head of a whole flock of goslings!

Boll weevils are little black bugs that invaded the United States from Mexico around 1890. They spread from Texas through the entire South, destroying the cotton crops. Utter poverty followed in the wake of the boll weevils, and Negro farm laborers were the chief sufferers. But the Negroes couldn't resist identifying themselves with the bug who was, like them, black and homeless.

> First time I seen the boll weevil,
> He's settin' on the square;
> Next time I seen him,
> He had his family there.

The "square," incidentally, refers to the shape of the cotton blossom. Through this song, the Negro says that he and his children will survive, no matter what their trials. When the white farmer tries putting the boll weevil in hot sand, the bug says, "I'll stand it like a man." The farmer tries ice, and the bug says, "Dis is mighty cool and nice." The boll weevil song has been a work song, a ballad, a blues and, in our own time, a popular record hit.

John and Alan Lomax, a father and son folklore team, found and recorded many old hollers and work songs in southern Negro prisons from 1933 to 1940. By that time, such songs were seldom sung in the outside world; but they were kept alive in prisons by the hard physical labor, loneliness and isolation of convict life. The Lomaxes made these recordings for the Archive of Folk Song of the Library of Congress.

They took portable recording equipment into penitentiaries in Mississippi and Arkansas. There they found convicts who still sang in a harsh vibrant style that reached back to slave days. The words the convicts used reflected their feelings about prison life. They sang about the long years away from home, the women they missed, the grueling labor, the monotonous food, the prison guards they called "captain."

Rhythmic work songs had a special importance on chain gangs. Bound together, the convicts *had* to move together. The old songs took their minds off their troubles—at least for a while. "If you don't sing, you sho' get worried," went one prison song. These songs gave the men a chance to express their true feelings and mock the white guards in ways that never would have been allowed in the ordinary exchanges of prison life. One of the best-known prison work songs went:

Take this hammer—*huh!*—carry it to the captain—*huh!*
Tell him I'm gone, tell him I'm gone—*huh!*

The song leader called out the lines, holding the word "captain" as long as he could—with a glance and a grin at the white guard—to give his buddies a little rest. The convicts swung their hammers in time to the song; the "*huh*" burst out in chorus—a violent grunt of exhaled breath at the end of each swing.

If he asks you—*huh!*—was I runnin'?—*huh!*
Tell him Ise flyin', tell him Ise flyin'—*huh!*

Prison songs were full of images of escape. In spite of armed guards and packs of bloodhounds, many convicts tried to escape, and a few made it. "Long John" was a legendary escapee, the hero of many a prison song. One version from a Texas prison farm set the pace for an axe gang.

It's a *long* John,
He's a *long* gone,
Like a *turkey* through the corn,
Through the *long* corn. . . .

The trains that passed the prisons were woven into these songs, too. The "Midnight Special" was a train that ran between Houston, Texas, and San Francisco and passed the Texas State Prison Farm at Sugarland on the way. This train, shining its "ever lovin' light" through the barred windows of the prison, worked into the convicts' dreams of freedom and their songs.

The singer who made many of these prison songs famous was Huddie (Leadbelly) Ledbetter. Leadbelly was a big, violent, magnetic man, twice convicted of murder, who spent many years in southern penitentiaries. He called himself the King of the Twelve-String Guitar; and he played and sang the songs of labor gangs and convicts better perhaps than anyone else.

Leadbelly was born on a farm in Louisiana about 1885, the son of a former slave. All through his childhood, Leadbelly heard the songs of country Negroes, remembered from slave days. He taught himself to play the guitar and the accordion and, while still a boy, played at Saturday night dances up and down the countryside. Later he wandered through Texas and the Delta lands, working on construction gangs, in lumber camps, and on the levees of the Mississippi. He learned many of his songs from Blind Lemon Jefferson, a Texas street singer and guitarist, who had a great stock of back country ballads and blues.

But most of Leadbelly's songs were learned or worked over during long terms in prison. He led a rough, brawling life and was often in trouble with the law. On chain gangs, he was lead man, pouring his great strength into swinging a pick deeper than anyone else and singing along with it. He had a big booming voice with a rough edge, and whether he was setting the pace for gang labor or singing just to relieve the loneliness and tedium of prison life, he sang with searing emotional power.

Singing got him out of jail twice. The first time, the governor of Texas heard him sing and released him from the state prison. But Leadbelly was soon back in the penitentiary —this time in Louisiana. John Lomax discovered him there when recording songs of the convicts for the Library of Congress and helped him get an audience with the governor of Louisiana. After hearing him sing, the governor gave Leadbelly a pardon and paroled him to Mr. Lomax. This was in 1934.

Leadbelly went north and during the years that followed was widely heard on the concert stage, in night clubs and on college campuses. He made hundreds of recordings for the Library of Congress archives and for commercial record companies. When he played and sang on the concert stage, he used no microphone, for his strong voice easily filled any hall.

For Leadbelly, singing came as naturally as breathing. He liked to twang his guitar and let the music rise—whether he was playing for a group of children in a hospital or for a millionaire's party. He was a roughneck who could be as gentle as a lamb, and he never lost his gusto and gift of hard laughter. In his music, he had absolute integrity. He sang and played Negro folk songs the way he remembered and felt them.

Among Leadbelly's best-known songs were "Good Night, Irene," and "Rock Island Line," both of which were taken up by other singers and widely popularized. He also sang "Take this Hammer," "The Gray Goose," and "John Henry," changing the lyrics and adding verses in the freewheeling style of true folk singers. When he died in 1949, he left a great legacy of song—field hollers, work songs, ballads and blues, that might otherwise have been forgotten. Folkways Records issued a memorial album of ninety-four of his songs.

Folk singers and jazz artists have been mining the rich ore of American Negro work songs for years, and there is no end in sight. We've had the original songs revived ("Michael Row de Boat Ashore"), or revised ("Boll Weevil Song"), or simply used as a springboard for a rocking ballad (Sam Cooke's song about a chain gang). In the straight jazz field, there's Nat Adderly's "Work Song," as played by brother Cannonball's quintet. And in concert jazz, we have Duke Ellington's introduction to his extended work "Black, Brown and Beige"—a work song passage in which the beat falls like hammer blows and the melody evokes the misery and grinding toil of slave days.

CHAPTER THREE

THE OLD TIME RELIGION

Ring Shouts to Spirituals

The religious music of the American Negro has always had a give-and-take relationship with jazz. Before jazz was born, hymns and work songs overlapped; so did spirituals and blues. In our own day, the strong beat and fervor of gospel singing in Negro Baptist and Methodist churches and in the Sanctified Sect have been absorbed into everything from rock-and-roll to concert jazz; and jazz, in turn, has worked its way back into the music of these churches.

Many a Negro jazz musician has been brought up on song sermons and rousing hymns. When Dizzy Gillespie was asked why vibraphonist Milt Jackson has such a fine sense of rhythm, he replied, "Why, man, he's Sanctified." Jackson, like Gillespie himself, was raised on the music of the Sanctified Church.

The story of American Negro religious music begins with the introduction of Christianity among the slaves. The Negroes brought many religious and musical traditions with them from West Africa. They were forbidden to practice their ancient religions here, for the slaveowners feared the powerful emotions unleashed by ritual drumming, chanting and dancing. The slaves had to find a safe channel through which to express their religious feelings. Christianity provided this channel and a refuge from the sorrows of slavery as well.

The old African ways of worship were not forgotten altogether, even when the Negroes wholeheartedly accepted the faith of their white masters. The strong pulse and repetition of West African religious ceremonies and even the trance state of "spirit possession" worked their way in acceptable guises into Christian services on southern plantations.

The most African of all such services was the "ring shout," a kind of shuffling dance with chanting and hand clapping, that followed prayer meetings in slave days. The slaves shuffled around and around in a ring, moving counterclockwise in accordance with West African custom. They were not allowed to dance in church, so they did not cross their legs. (The Bible describes dancing as a crossing of legs.) They sang as they shuffled and clapped out a powerful rhythmic accompaniment.

The words of shout songs were taken from Bible stories or white hymns. One of the favorites went:

> I can't stay behind, my Lord,
> I can't stay behind!
> Dere's room enough, room enough,
> Room enough, in Heab'n, my Lord,
> Room enough, room enough,
> I can't stay behind. . . .

There was more rhythm than melody in these songs. They were originally chanted in leader-chorus form. Sometimes the dancers sang; sometimes tired dancers stood at the side of the room and accompanied their shuffling brethren with singing and hand clapping.

Shouts started slowly but picked up speed and intensity as

they went along. The same body movements, the same musical phrases, were repeated over and over, with hypnotic effect on the dancers. The monotonous thud thud of feet on bare floor boards was like the beating of African drums. After hours of shuffling and chanting, many of the dancers became "possessed" and screamed and flung themselves about in a transport of religious ecstasy.

Many of the basic qualities of the ring shout can be found in the song-sermons of Negro churches. The song-sermon is a way of preaching that wavers between speech and music, that has a blues sound and a powerful beat and that is punctuated by responses from the congregation.

In slave times, Negro elders told stories from the Bible or led their brethren in hymns a few lines at a time. The congregation would repeat these lines in a chorus, or they would break in with groans and shouts—"Amen!" "That's right!" "Yes, My Lord!" This was the old leader-chorus form, remembered from Africa. It was the form of the work song, the form the slaves fell into naturally when they sang as a group.

White churches in this country in colonial times had a similar custom that was called "lining out." White preachers "lined out" psalms, a few bars at a time, which the members of the congregation repeated. This custom originated in the British Isles at a time when few people could read, and it took root here wherever church members couldn't read or were too poor to buy hymn books. It spread from New England to backwoods churches in the South and West. Negroes heard "lined out" hymns and were influenced by them.

When a Negro preacher delivered a song-sermon, he spoke, chanted and sang, picking up speed and fervor as he went along—his flock cutting in and out with sharp cries in perfect rhythm or with short lines of melody. A great folk preacher could start with a fixed text and then improvise, never losing the beat, building up tremendous emotional effect through repetition. Alan Lomax suggests that the Negro preacher was familiar with the devices of old southern orators —but used them like a voodoo priest.

Two good recordings of Negro song-sermons are "Dry Bones" (Jazz, Folkways, Vol. I) and "I'm Going to Heaven" (History of Classic Jazz, Riverside, RLP 12-112), both with the Reverend J. M. Gates and congregation. In them the preacher intones the sermon slowly at first and then builds up to a driving chant as the responses burst from the congregation. A single soprano voice detaches itself from this chorus, in each record, and soars in a beautiful slow sad counterpoint to the hoarse exhortations of the preacher.

These song-sermons echo old field hollers, work songs, and ring shouts—all blended with Biblical stories and hymns taught the slaves by their white masters. The song-sermon is still very much with us—a living reminder of the sources of jazz. Such sermons can be heard in Negro evangelical churches, and they are often broadcast over radio stations that reach the Negro populations of big cities.

American Negro religious music reached its peak in spirituals, beautiful songs of faith and hope. Such songs as "Go Down, Moses," "Deep River" and "Swing Low, Sweet Chariot" are known and loved by millions. Spirituals have been called the most impressive body of music so far produced by America.

Spirituals developed later than ring shouts and song-sermons. They had their great heyday during the last twenty years of slavery. By that time, Methodists and Baptists had won many converts among the slaves. Negro spirituals show the strong influence of these white churches. They also show the deep impression made on the slaves by the Great Revival meetings of the early nineteenth century. White spirituals came into existence at great religious jamborees held in open fields and tents. Poor white people and Negroes flocked to these camp meetings. They sang fiery shouting hymns, quite different from the old restrained and doleful music of Puritan churches. White and Negro spirituals borrowed from each other, mixing and blending until no one knows for sure which music more strongly influenced the other.

Early Negro spirituals were simple melodies passed back and forth between a leader and chorus a line at a time. "Oh, Wasn't Dat a Wide Ribber?" (which is close in form and melody to a Nigerian chant, "Oh! The Long Lances") is such a song:

> *Leader:* Oh, de ribber of Jordan is deep and wide,
> *Chorus:* One more ribber to cross.
> *Leader:* I don't know how to go on de other side,
> *Chorus:* One more ribber to cross.
> *Leader:* Oh, you got Jesus, hold him fast,
> *Chorus:* One more ribber to cross. . . .

"Swing Low, Sweet Chariot" is another song in which the chorus chimes in, over and over, with a single line, "Comin' for to carry me home."

Good examples of early spirituals have been recorded for the Archive of American Folk Song (Library of Congress, AAFS L 3).

The slaves seldom used white hymns in their original form. Spirituals evolved from fragments of these hymns—single lines of text or a few bars of melody that appealed to the Negroes and that they repeated and used as a base for improvisation.

They embellished their spirituals with haunting vocal effects —the slides, swoops, quavers, and slightly off-pitch notes that were heard in hollers and work songs, and that would be heard again in the blues.

Most important, they transformed the material they borrowed from white hymns by changing the rhythm, shifting the accent from the strong to the weak beats. Spirituals are syncopated. It can be said without irreverence that these noble songs "swing."

It's almost impossible to hear a spiritual and sit still. Negro congregations swayed their heads and bodies as they sang spirituals, clapped their hands and tapped their feet. Body swaying marked off the regular beat or surge; and head swaying marked off the surge in shorter waves. Hand clapping accented the off-beats; foot tapping the strong beats.

The words of the spirituals record the deepest thoughts and experiences of the Negroes.

The teachings of the Bible helped them to endure slavery. They trusted that God would save them, as He saved Daniel from the lion's den and the Hebrew children from the fiery furnace. They identified themselves with the Hebrews, who were slaves, too, and who were delivered out of bondage in Egypt. One of the most stirring of the spirituals is "Go Down, Moses," which deals with this theme. This spiritual is cast in a combination of call-and-response and choral forms:

> *Leader:* When Israel was in Egypt land,
> *Response:* Let my people go.
> *Leader:* Oppressed so hard, she could not stand,
> *Response:* Let my people go.
> *Chorus:* Go down, Moses,
>   Way down in Egypt land,
>   Tell old Pharaoh
>   To let my people go.

This beautiful spiritual uses the majestic language of the Old Testament. The texts of many other spirituals come from the New Testament. Jesus was called "Massa Jesus" and "King Jesus," and the crucifixion and resurrection were favored topics. "He Never Said a Mumblin' Word" recounts the story of the crucifixion in a folk style that is deeply moving:

> Dey crucified my Lord,
> And he never said a mumblin' word—
> Dey nailed him to de tree,
> And he never said a mumblin' word—
> Dey pierced him in de side,
> And he never said a mumblin' word—
> The blood came twinklin' down,
> And he never said a mumblin' word. . . .

Most spirituals dealt with the real woes of the slaves, so much so that they were sometimes called "sorrow songs." "Nobody Knows the Trouble I've Seen" is a sorrow song; so is "Sometimes I Feel Like a Motherless Child." Such songs are never sentimental or theatrical. They speak of profound feelings in the direct, concise style of great poetry. What better image could one find for the slave than a "motherless child"? He had been uprooted from his homeland, separated from his family and tribe and stripped of his identity. When he sang "Sometimes I feel I never been borned," he expressed the full weight of his misery.

But in the midst of his woes, the slave created another kind of spiritual that bubbled over with warmth and friendliness. In these songs, man and deity were on easy familiar terms:

> When I get to heab'n, gonna be at ease,
> Me an' my God gonna do as we please. . . .

Heaven, in such spirituals, was a kind of happy picnic grounds. The slaves pictured themselves dressed in fine robes and starry crowns, invited to rest at last:

> "Set down, servant." "I can't sit down. . . .
> My soul's so happy that I can't sit down."

"Great Gettin' Up Mornin'," with its rousing refrain, "Fare thee well, fare thee well!" was another joyful hymn. "Joshua

Fit de Battle of Jericho" was in the same jubilant mood. Spirituals like these were later called jubilees.

Some spirituals had double meanings known only to Negroes. In the years before the Civil War, thousands of slaves escaped along the "Underground Railroad," which, of course, was not a railroad at all but a chain of hiding places in the homes of white sympathizers. According to legend, the slaves spoke of these escapes in a disguised way through their spirituals. When they sang of "Beulah Land," they meant both "heaven" and "freedom." The Biblical land, of Canaan, often mentioned in spirituals, came to mean Canada.

A Negro woman named Harriet Tubman, herself an escaped slave, was a famous heroine of the Underground Railroad movement. She slipped back into the South many times and led hundreds of her people to freedom in Canada. Although the slave states offered a $10,000 reward for her capture, she was never caught; nor were any of the Negroes she helped along the escape route. It's thought that the great spiritual, "Go Down, Moses," which is often called the Marseillaise of slavery, came to refer to Harriet Tubman; that she was the "Moses" of this stirring song, and that the Negroes were the "Israelites," the slaveowners "Pharaoh," and the South "Egypt."

On the eve of the Civil War, the spirit of rebellion among the Negroes was expressed more and more openly. Songs that seemed merely wistful longings for the afterlife turned into battle hymns. "My Father, How Long?" began:

> My Father, how long . . .
> Poor sinner suffer here?

But the words soon changed:

> We'll soon be free . . .
> De Lord will call us home,

We'll fight for liberty . . .
When de Lord will call us home.

Negroes in South Carolina were jailed for singing this spiritual at the outbreak of the war.

When the war was over and the slaves freed, spirituals all but disappeared. White southerners had for many years taken these beautiful songs for granted, and few white men had tried to write them down. The Negroes, themselves, of course, didn't know how to write music; and they had no record of their spirituals except in their memories. When they became free men, they tried to forget these old songs that were so painfully associated with slavery. During the first few years after the Civil War, both whites and Negroes seemed willing to let spirituals die.

Happily, a few historians and musicologists understood how important it was to save this music for future generations. The federal government took a hand through the Freedmen's Bureau, which was created to aid emancipated slaves. With the help of this bureau, scholars gathered together work songs and spirituals of Negroes in the Port Royal Islands off the coast of South Carolina. The result was *Slave Songs of the United States*, the first book of its kind, which was published in 1867. The editors collected a large number of songs that might otherwise have been lost forever and presented them in a sympathetic and scholarly way.

A few years later, a group of young Negro students from the Fisk School in Nashville, Tennessee, gave a great boost to the survival and popularity of the spiritual in an extraordinary concert tour. The Fisk singers started on tour in 1871 to raise money for their college. They were induced to sing spirituals by their teacher, a white man, George L. White, although they were at first reluctant to sing these songs in public.

Fisk was then a desperately poor school. It had been

founded by missionaries of the Congregational Church three years after Abraham Lincoln signed the Emancipation Proclamation. In the early days, the teachers faced what seemed a hopeless struggle. The students who flocked to the school were almost all ex-slaves. Few of them could read or write. There was little money for books, pencils or paper—or for fuel to heat the abandoned army barracks in which classes were held.

By 1871, the missionaries had succeeded in raising the educational level bit by bit, until they were conducting some college classes and were beginning to train Negro teachers; but the financial plight of the school was worse than ever. Mr. White, who was the treasurer of Fisk as well as the music teacher, conceived the idea of taking some of his students on a concert tour to raise a little money for the institution.

The Fisk chorus was made up of nine young men and women, seven of them former slaves. They set out in borrowed clothes with just enough money to get them to Cincinnati, where a great exposition was in progress. They were completely unknown to the white audiences they hoped to conquer.

Things went badly at first. At Cincinnati, they sang such songs as "Annie Laurie" and "Home, Sweet Home." George White wanted them to include some spirituals in the program, but the young singers resisted. They were afraid that white people would laugh at the dialect; besides, they couldn't think of "slave songs" as serious music suitable for the concert stage. Audiences at the Cincinnati Exposition weren't interested in hearing Negroes sing "Home, Sweet Home," and little money came in. The Fisk singers moved on to other Ohio towns with the same discouraging results.

A change came at Oberlin, when the Fisk students went to a Congregational religious conference. They sat at the back of the church where the meeting took place, waiting for a chance to sing during a lull in the program. They were weary and dispirited. When their chance finally came, late in the afternoon, Mr. White whispered to them to start singing, very softly, the old spiritual, "Steal Away to Jesus." Too tired to argue, they sang:

> The trumpet sounds within-a my soul,
> I ain't got long to stay here. . . .

The audience was made up of white northerners, most of whom had never heard a spiritual before. They were deeply moved by the beautiful melody, the simple poetry and deep feeling of the music. They didn't laugh. Many of them cried. The young Negro singers were asked to sing encore after encore.

This was the turning point in a tour that was to make musical history. The group became the Fisk Jubilee Singers. Singing such spirituals as "Roll, Jordan, Roll" and "Turn Back Pharaoh's Army," they created a sensation in New York. The newspapers reported that "gray-haired men wept like children" at the "weird and plaintive hymns." One of the papers called their songs "the only true native school of American music." Then came a highly successful tour of New England. To cap these triumphs, the Fisk singers were invited to sing for President Grant at the White House.

In 1873, the group went to Europe. This junket was successful beyond the wildest dreams of George White and his Jubilee Singers. In England, they sang before Queen Victoria and the Prince of Wales, dined with Gladstone and had their portrait painted by the Queen's favorite artist. In Russia, they sang for the Czarina. Between these encounters with the great and famous, they gave many concerts for the plain people of the countries through which they traveled, for children and workers, the sick in hospitals, inmates of prisons.

The people of Europe responded to the beauty of the spirituals and to their deep feeling, whether they understood the words or not. Spirituals spoke to them in the language of universal human experience and emotion—the same language that would take another American music, jazz, around the globe several generations later.

When the Fisk Jubilee Singers finished their tour, they had been on the road for seven years and earned $150,000 for their college. This was enough money to buy a beautiful campus for Fisk and to build a fine four-story "Jubilee Hall."

They had helped in a dramatic way to preserve spirituals and to reawaken the Negroes themselves to the value of this music. They had introduced half the world to certain characteristics of American Negro folk music—to the syncopated rhythm, the call and response form, the free weaving of improvised lines into the basic pattern of melody. They accustomed the ears of white listeners to the strange swoops and glides of slave singing and to the haunting off-pitch notes and quavers.

All this paved the way for blues and jazz.

Gospel music came much later than spirituals. Gospels are not folk songs. They are written pieces that first came into use in Negro churches about 1925. They hark back, like spirituals, to the cry of lonely field hands in slave days; to the rhythms of railroad crews and chain gangs; to the spellbinding sermons of Negro preachers and the ecstatic hand clapping and foot stamping of Deep South congregations. But they have roots in jazz, too.

One of the first composers of gospel songs was Thomas A. Dorsey of the Pilgrim Baptist Church in Chicago. Before he turned to church music, Mr. Dorsey was a piano accompanist for Ma Rainey, a great early blues singer. He was well known, too, as a player of joyous rocking piano tunes; and he carried the happy spirit and powerful beat of these pieces into his gospel songs.

Gospel music is always joyous, unlike spirituals, which more often express the depths of human suffering. Mahalia Jackson explains the happy quality of her gospel singing this way: "There is something in the Bible that tells how I feel about all this. It's from the sixty-sixth Psalm, where David said, 'Make a joyous noise unto the Lord,' and then he said, 'Sing with a loud voice.'"

Miss Jackson, greatest of present-day gospel singers, was born in 1911 in New Orleans and absorbed in her childhood the music that burst from the streets and honky-tonks of that pleasure-loving city. She was brought up in an intensely religious atmosphere, but she could hardly avoid hearing the "sinful" music that sounded from street bands by day and rocked the dance halls at night. She also heard the blues records of Bessie Smith, which made a deep impression on her.

Mahalia came from poor hard-working people. Her father was a dock worker and barber on weekdays and a preacher on Sundays. Mahalia started to sing in his church when she was five years old. There was no such thing as gospel music in those days. She sang spirituals and old Baptist hymns.

Mahalia left school after the eighth grade to help her family by working as a baby nurse. By that time, her beautiful voice soared above the others in the choir, and many people came to the small church expressly to hear her. She came to the attention of jazz musicians, too, and she had offers to work with them; but she refused, as she was to refuse over and over during her career, to sing songs that did not jibe with her deep religious convictions.

When Mahalia was sixteen she went to Chicago. She joined the Great Salem Baptist Church there soon after her arrival and quickly became a soloist in the choir. Written gospel music was just becoming popular, and the director of the choir formed a quintet of gospel singers around Mahalia which was soon in great demand at other churches and revival meetings. Mahalia worked as a maid to earn a living and spent every spare moment in church work and gospel singing.

She became famous for her big warm contralto voice—of remarkable range and flexibility—and for the moving sincerity of her performances. She decorated the simple gospel tunes with breathtaking glides and swoops.

As time went on, Miss Jackson was able to devote herself completely to singing. She traveled widely and made gospel records that were phenomenal best-sellers. The records were intended at first for the Negro trade; but soon white people were buying them, too. They knew they were hearing superb examples of a new and powerfully rhythmical kind of Negro music. Mahalia's fame spread through concert tours here and abroad and through many memorable performances on radio and television.

Mahalia Jackson is a living example of the overlapping relation between American Negro religious music and jazz. She never sings in night clubs. All her songs have religious themes. Nevertheless, she belongs in the company of great blues singers. Like Bessie Smith, whom she resembles in her majestic physical appearance and velvety contralto voice, she can slide in and around notes to create a solid blue tonality. Her phrasing and rhythmic sense are rooted in jazz.

Blues are the closest link between Negro church music and jazz. Blues singer Alberta Hunter remarked in Shapiro and Hentoff's *Hear Me Talkin' To Ya:* "The blues are like spirituals, almost sacred. When we sing blues, we're singing out our hearts, we're singing out our feelings."

These feelings are what give jazz its extra dimension—the depth of emotion that goes beyond fresh sounds and exciting rhythms. The fiery faith of the old-time Negro sermon, the sadness and poetry of the spiritual, the rousing joy of the gospel song—all have helped make jazz what it is.

CHAPTER FOUR

THE RHYTHM MAKERS

Minstrel Men and Ragtimers

In the middle of the nineteenth century, this country was swept by a rage for a new kind of entertainment based on the music and jokes of southern Negroes. White actors blackened their faces with burnt cork and did imitations of plantation songs and dances. They joked in broad dialect and played at being ignorant happy-go-lucky "darkies." This was the beginning of the minstrel show, a form of entertainment that was to reign supreme on American stages for more than fifty years.

Few people alive today have ever seen a genuine minstrel show. It's hard to imagine the important role that such shows once played in American life. Traveling minstrel troupes reached cities and hamlets, farm centers and frontier towns. They brought a glittering, tuneful, slapstick world to audiences who were starved for entertainment. The arrival of a minstrel troupe, advertised with gaudy posters, sent ripples of excitement through the sleepiest village. Everyone who could earn, beg or borrow the price of admission went to the show.

All early minstrel players were white men; but at the end of the Civil War, Negroes formed their own companies modeled on those already in the field. Negro players, ironically enough, found themselves imitating their imitators. With greatly talented performers—both white and Negro—in the business, minstrelsy boomed as never before. Minstrel men saturated the country with American Negro music and educated the public in the Negro manner of singing, dancing and playing instruments.

Minstrel shows were inspired by slave entertainments on southern plantations. It was the custom on some plantations to call groups of slaves to the "Big House" to amuse visitors with songs, jigs and music played on homemade instruments. Sometimes these slaves traveled to neighboring plantations to perform at parties. In this way, white people began to know and appreciate the special treatment Negroes gave to songs and dances.

The slaves had no access to European musical instruments. Drums were forbidden to them; but they accompanied themselves with bone clappers, tambourines and homemade banjos. "Bones" were small polished sheep bones which were rattled between the fingers. Tambourines resembled African finger drums, and they were tapped and shaken to vary the rhythm. Both bones and tambourines found their way into minstrel shows. From the earliest days of minstrelsy, the two featured comedians, or end men, were called "Mr. Bones" and "Mr. Tambo."

The favorite plantation instrument was the banjo. It was crudely made in slave quarters, and like the tambourine, it probably had African antecedents. The banjo gave its distinctive sound and mood to the minstrel era. The lighthearted syncopation created on the banjo by slave musicians set the pace for minstrel songs and dance, and eventually touched off a ragtime craze that swept the nation.

The first minstrel man on record was a young German musician named Gottlieb Graupner, who arrived in Charleston, South Carolina, in 1795. Graupner learned to imitate the Negro music he heard around Charleston. In 1799, he blackened his face with burnt cork, billed himself as "The Gay Negro Boy" and sang Negro songs in an interlude between the acts at the Federal Street Theatre in Boston. The act was a hit. But Graupner's real interest was classical music. He soon abandoned blackface make-up and Negro dialect to organize the Boston Philharmonic Society.

Graupner had many successors who did blackface imitations, often between the acts of "legitimate" shows. One of the best known was Thomas (Jim Crow) Rice, whose imitation of a Negro stablehand brought him national and even international fame. About 1830 Rice was acting in a play in Louisville, Kentucky. At a livery stable near the theater, he saw an old crippled Negro do a little comic dance. As the Negro danced, he sang:

> Wheel about, turn about,
>   Do jis' so,
> An' ebery time I wheel about,
>   I jump Jim Crow!

Rice learned the song. He blackened his face, dressed in tattered clothes, and sang this song in an intermission. He was a talented mimic, and he turned and hopped like a crow and crookedly flapped his arms, just as he had seen the old man do. The audience went wild and called him back for twenty encores. "Jump Jim Crow" swept the country and traveled to England.

The first minstrel company was put together in 1842 by an Irish-American backwoodsman named Daniel Decatur Emmett. Emmett and three other performers made up the original troupe. They played violin, tambourine, bones, and banjo. They blackened their faces and dressed in long-tailed blue suits, which became the standard uniform of all minstrels. Emmett called his players the Virginia Minstrels, and the cast grew as they traveled and prospered.

Emmett was a gifted composer, and in 1859 he composed "Dixie-land," which he billed as an "Ethiopian Walk-Around." This is the same "Dixie" that became the battle song of the Confederacy—a use certainly not intended by its northern composer.

As minstrels took shape, they developed a standard routine. The "interlocutor," who acted as master of ceremonies and straight man, welcomed the audience. Then the end men came bouncing out of the wings with a flourish of bones and tambourines. The orchestra struck up a lively medley, and the cast took seats in a semicircle facing the audience. The show began with jokes and slapstick antics by the end men, and music and songs by the whole company.

The second part of the show, in which the soloists performed, was called the "olio" from the Spanish "olla" meaning mixture. The climax was usually a kind of hoedown in which each dancer did his specialty while the other members of the cast gathered around and sang and clapped their hands. The olio, with its series of solo acts, was the forerunner of vaudeville and variety shows.

The olio was often followed by a playlet which was a wild parody of some well-known stage offering. *Uncle Tom's Cabin*, in its day, was a favorite subject for minstrel burlesque. Even in this part of the show, songs and dances would be introduced if there was the least excuse.

The smash finish was the grand walk-around by the whole cast. They circled the stage in a high-stepping dance called the cakewalk. In this number, the dancers mimicked the elegant dress and courtly gestures of the southern gentry. The cakewalk had originated in slave quarters to poke fun at these highfalutin' manners. When minstrels introduced this dance to the general public, it became a national craze. There were cakewalk contests, with cakes as prizes, in dance halls and cabarets. New York society took up the fad, and there were cakewalks at every ball.

The favorite solo dance of the minstrels was the buck and wing, ancestor of present-day tap dancing. Like the cakewalk, the buck and wing goes back to plantation days, in this case to folk dances that the slaves picked up from Irish and Scottish settlers.

Many minstrel songs can be traced back to early Negro sources. One of the most popular of all such tunes was "Turkey in the Straw," which goes back to a popular song of the early nineteenth century called "Zip Coon," and before *that* to a Negro song, "Natchez Under the Hill," heard on Mississippi River boats.

White composers tried to catch the melodic and rhythmic spirit of this music to fill the minstrels' demand for new material. Stephen Foster was the most successful. He wrote some of his best-loved songs for minstrels. "Oh, Susanna!" "Swanee River," "De Camptown Races" and "Old Black Joe" were minstrel songs.

Foster was born in Pennsylvania and had little direct contact with the South or slave music. Nevertheless, his songs caught the feeling of Negro folk music with a poignant beauty and simplicity. He wrote lyrics for his minstrel songs in Negro dialect and called them, in the fashion of his day, "Ethiopian."

Most of Foster's minstrel songs were written in mid-nineteenth century. "Oh, Susanna!" which was first introduced by minstrels, became the theme song of the Gold Rush. Its gay rhythm and jaunty lyrics suited the mood of the '49ers in their headlong dash across the continent. "De Camptown Races," which was written a little later, had the same happy driving beat and was popular in and out of minstrels. Both these songs were clearly inspired by the lighthearted side of Negro music; but Foster also drew on the plaintive haunting strain in slave songs to produce "Old Black Joe" and "Swanee River."

Like the folk music that inspired them, Foster's songs lend themselves naturally to jazz. They have a basic ragtime flavor and the same simple harmonic structure as early jazz pieces. "Swanee River" and "Jeannie with the Light Brown Hair" are two Foster melodies that have often been used by jazz musicians.

After the Civil War, Negroes, too, began to write music for minstrel shows. James A. Bland was the best known of these composers. His songs were catchy and melodious and suggested European ballads more than the work songs and spirituals of plantation days.

Bland grew up in Washington, D. C., in the early years after Emancipation when many Negro families wanted to forget the music associated with slavery. When he was in his teens, he started to play the banjo in spite of his parents' objections. He enrolled at Howard University but soon left to join the Haverly Colored Minstrels, one of the few all-Negro shows that successfully toured the North.

The players in the Haverly Minstrels were resplendent in silk frock coats and top hats, and they wore diamond stickpins in their ties. Like white minstrels, they blackened their faces with cork and joked in the uneducated dialect that was supposed to be a humorous imitation of plantation speech. Bland soon won a featured role in this assembly. He was a talented singer and banjo player; and he could write songs that were much like Stephen Foster's in their lyrical appeal.

Bland's first big hit was the familiar "Carry Me Back to Old Virginny." A great favorite with both white and Negro minstrels, it eventually became the official song of the state of Virginia. He followed this success with another, "In the

Evening by the Moonlight," a sentimental ballad that has been harmonized by many generations of barbershop quartets.

The Haverly Minstrels traveled to London, where they had a long run at Her Majesty's Theatre. Bland introduced there his own song, "Oh, Dem Golden Slippers," which became the rage. He returned to England many times during the next twenty years and was one of the favorite entertainers of the Prince of Wales, later King Edward VII.

Bland wrote several hundred tunes during his lifetime but often neglected to copyright them. He earned large sums of money at times, but like Foster, he died alone and poor.

William C. Handy, "Father of the Blues," is another famous graduate of Negro minstrels. In the 1890's, Handy led a big band that traveled with Mahara's Minstrels, an all-Negro company under the management of three Irish brothers. By this time, Negro performers had washed off the burnt cork; but the old minstrel routines still delighted the nation's audiences.

Handy's travels with Mahara's Minstrels brought him into contact with the most gifted Negro singers and instrumentalists of the day; with Negro audiences whose ties to old plantation music were still strong; and with roaming street musicians who sang of heroes, convicts and faithless lovers. This was the rich ore that Handy mined for his blues.

The vogue of minstrels began to decline around 1900. Vaudeville arrived and borrowed many of its ideas from minstrelsy—and many of its performers, too. Then movies and radio delivered all but final blows. Only a few small minstrel companies struggled on after World War I. The great traditions of the minstrel show passed into the hands of the stars of a new amusement world.

A basic effect of minstrel music was that it prepared American ears for jazz. It introduced a wide audience to the African strain—however diluted—that ran through the minstrel version of slave songs and instrument playing. It also paved the way for ragtime, which if not exactly jazz, was a close relative.

Ragtime started in the late 1890's when minstrels had already hit their peak and were beginning to lose ground. It was a cheerful syncopated music that had close ties to the fast "raggedy" banjo tunes played for jigs and cakewalks in minstrel shows. As minstrels waned, ragtime became a musical craze that swept the country in a great tide of tinkling rhythm.

Ragtime is not an ancestor of jazz, as is sometimes supposed. It took shape in the Midwest at about the same time that a true jazz music was emerging in New Orleans and elsewhere; and for some years the two styles ran more or less separate courses. They overlapped at times and finally merged completely. In its heyday (1897 to 1917), ragtime easily eclipsed all other popular music. It jingled in cabarets and dance halls, and in the nation's parlors—where the pianola, a mechanical piano that played paper rolls, reigned supreme.

At the heart of ragtime is syncopation, which means simply that the normally weak beats are accented. Ragtime began as piano music in which the right hand played a rippling syncopation and the left hand a steady unsyncopated marching beat. This was a formula that could be applied to almost any piece of music. Unlike New Orleans music, which depended from the beginning on the improvising talent of the players, ragtime could be played as written by any musician who could read notes.

Sedalia, Missouri, is called the birthplace of ragtime because it was the headquarters of Scott Joplin, greatest of ragtime composers. Joplin was a wandering keyboard artist who learned his first rags from an old German-American honky-tonk pianist. He drifted to Sedalia in the 1890's and started to write a long series of brilliant and complicated rags, of which the "Maple Leaf Rag," named after a Sedalia café, is the most famous. Joplin was a serious student of composition, and he dreamed of making ragtime a great national music. During his lifetime, he published more than fifty ragtime piano pieces, wrote two ragtime operas, and did an instruction book called "School of Ragtime."

St. Louis was another ragtime center, where early pianists played Scott Joplin's pieces and wrote rags of their own. Tom Turpin, a jovial 300-pound saloonkeeper, was the originator of a fast showy St. Louis school of ragtime. James Scott, a more retiring type known as the Little Professor, wrote original and surprisingly vigorous numbers, including a longtime favorite, "Grace and Beauty."

Joplin, Turpin and Scott all happened to be Negroes, but they drew more heavily on the traditions of European music than on Negro folk sources. Only the smallest traces of Negro work songs or spirituals can be found in their compositions. Many white composers, too, worked successfully in the ragtime field. Joseph Lamb, who wrote "American Beauty Rag," is the best known.

The general public first heard ragtime around the turn of the century at a series of world's fairs in Chicago, Omaha, Buffalo and St. Louis. Joplin wrote a special rag, "The Cascades," in honor of the water display on the Chicago Fair grounds. Ragtime playing competitions drew great crowds to the midway of the St. Louis Exposition. The rhythms of the new music were so infectious and danceable that they became a coast-to-coast craze. The publishers of popular music, who had their offices along "Tin Pan Alley," a strip of Broadway in New York City, turned out a steady stream of ragtime tunes. These were inferior to the works of the St. Louis and Sedalia pioneers but much easier to play. The sale of sheet music boomed, and the newest rags were hawked on every streetcorner.

Ragtime burst from every beer hall and saloon, from small-town bandstands, and even from merry-go-rounds and circus calliopes. When silent movies began, every movie house had a ragtime pianist who played along with the films.

Rag tunes set the pace for ballroom dancing, too. The cake-walk was the first big dance fad of the ragtime era, and it was followed by the two-step and a whole series of energetic dances with names borrowed from the animal kingdom—the Turkey Trot, Bunny Hug, Camel Walk and Kangaroo Dip.

The dance craze was helped along by Vernon and Irene Castle, who were the dancing idols of the American stage in the years just preceding World War I. The Castles created many of their dance hits to ragtime and thereby influenced the dances of the nation. They influenced dancing and musical tastes abroad, too, for they appeared with great success in London and Paris.

Ragtime was not altogether new to the capitals of Europe, for John Philip Sousa, the March King, who made tours abroad beginning in 1900, always sandwiched a few ragtime tunes in between conventional military numbers. Minstrel men and vaudeville artists, too, made American syncopation familiar to European audiences.

The first serious composers to use ragtime were Europeans. The French composer, Debussy, used minstrel themes in the "Golliwog's Cakewalk," written in 1908. Ten years later, Stravinsky wove syncopated dance rhythms into "Ragtime for Eleven Solo Instruments."

While ragtime was educating European ears it was also making new inroads at home. Some time before World War I ragtime piano was recorded for the first time on paper rolls. These were long sheets of paper cut with thousands of oblong holes that corresponded to the keys pressed down by a recording pianist. They were rolled into cylinders and sold as records are today.

It was great fun to put a ragtime roll on the old player piano and pump away at the pedals as ghostly fingers raced up and down the keyboard. Joplin, Scott, Lamb and other important ragtime figures made many rolls that demonstrated the vigor and technical brilliance of the best ragtime. As business boomed, the piano roll companies hired second-rate players who could rag any tune that came along.

An important part of the ragtime story is what happened to this music in New Orleans. Ragtime pianists were in great demand in the bars and honky-tonks of Storyville, the city's night-life district. Ferdinand (Jelly Roll) Morton, the famous New Orleans pianist, was a master of ragtime rhythm, but he gave it something extra—the New Orleans touch. His early records show what happened when the ragtime of Joplin, which was rooted in traditional European music, collided with Afro-American influences in New Orleans. Jelly Roll could play the "Maple Leaf Rag" in Joplin's own ragtime style; but he could also play it in a slower blues-tinged style that had more swing and flow.

New Orleans bands, too, had a ragtime tradition. The white musicians of the Reliance Brass Band, organized in New Orleans in 1892, played ragtime part of the time; so did the Negro players with Buddy Bolden and King Oliver. Musicians who could read notes used sheet music; those who could not read, improvised their own freewheeling versions of standard ragtime pieces.

The Dixieland jazz style that came out of New Orleans preserves to this day the flavor of the ragtime era. Dixieland bands still play old ragtime favorites, such as "Muskrat Ramble," "Original Dixieland One Step" and "Ostrich Walk." There is an infusion, too, of blues and spirituals; but the overall tone of Dixieland harks back to the days of cheerful syncopation.

There are several schools of thought about just what constitutes Dixieland. Some jazz historians feel that the term may be properly applied only to the style of certain white bands, notably the Original Dixieland Jazz Band and the New Orleans Rhythm Kings, who popularized a New Orleans type of ragtime. Others feel that the tag Dixieland may be loosely applied to any jazz played in the New Orleans manner—which includes the work of pioneer jazzmen, Negro and white, and their musical heirs of the Dixieland revival. Louis Armstrong calls his own musical style Dixieland.

Ragtime was also handed down through a line of great jazz pianists who only gradually and reluctantly gave up the old syncopations. Luckey Roberts, a Philadelphia-born ragtimer of legendary talent influenced James P. Johnson, "grandfather of Harlem piano," who in turn influenced Fats Waller—and just about every other jazz pianist of note in our times.

Johnson's story, like Armstrong's, spans almost the whole history of jazz. He began playing ragtime in Harlem cellars for cakewalk contests and the quadrille—a dance that was the ancestor of the Lindy Hop. This was long before World War I. Until his death in 1955, Johnson continued to love and play ragtime, although he was equally at home in other styles—from "stride," which he himself launched, to classical. Johnson is best remembered today as the composer of the "Charleston"; but the work that was close to his heart was a brilliant and extremely difficult ragtime concerto which was never performed.

These were the main streams of jazz music into which ragtime merged—into the Dixieland band style and Harlem piano. By 1917, the year that Scott Joplin died, ragtime as a separate and distinct popular music was finished. The strict, beautifully constructed rags of Joplin and his friends were forgotten; and the Tin Pan Alley tunes that had taken over now sounded corny and monotonous.

The phonograph moved into American parlors, and the player piano moved out. Piano rolls were stacked to gather dust in attic corners or in the warehouses of recording companies that were caught with stock on hand at the end of the boom. The fine old-time flavor of the ragtime era has been preserved, however, on LP records (Riverside RLP 12-110 and RLP 12-126). These are recordings of the work of the great early ragtimers, transferred from the original player rolls.

When the ragtime era ended, the stage was set for a new chapter in the history of American music.

CHAPTER FIVE

THE BLUES STORY

Folk Poetry in Music

Most people think of the blues as a sad, low-down, earthy kind of music with a strong beat. To the jazz musician, the blues means something quite different. He sees the blues as a particular kind of musical framework that lends itself wonderfully to jazz invention and improvisation. As singer Jimmy Rushing puts it, the blues is the base of jazz, "like the foundation of a building."

The blues came before jazz by quite a few years. There are plenty of fanciful song lyrics about the "birth of the blues," but few facts about when and how these songs originated. Blueslike songs were certainly known in slave days. Old Negro work songs, good-time music and spirituals all had a "bluesy" sound. But it seems clear that no real blues appeared until the end of the Civil War when Negro and white music began to have a greater impact on each other than ever before.

Early blues singers gathered together the haunting melodies of slave days and imposed a new order on them. The raw materials with which they worked came from the old reservoir of American Negro folk songs; from a way of singing and a way of looking at life ingrained through two-and-a-half centuries of slavery. But the structure of the blues came from white music.

The first professional blues singers were men. They were street musicians who wandered through the South with guitars slung over their shoulders. They sang country blues in a harsh, intense, shouting style that was close to the hollering of slave days. They told their adventures and misadventures in a twelve-bar form, setting the pattern of the blues for all time. The lyrics of their songs were mournful, but they also expressed a stoical humor:

> If your house catch on fire, Lord, and
>   there ain't no water around,
> If your house catch on fire, Lord, and
>   there ain't no water around,
> Throw your trunk out the window, and let
>   the shack burn down.

Women blues singers began to travel the minstrel and tent show circuits and to sing in theaters and cabarets in the early 1900's. They took the harsh edges off the country blues and turned the lyrics almost entirely to love troubles. This was the beginning of classic or city blues, a field dominated for many years by Negro women.

Blues flourished on the sidewalks and in the dance halls of Negro neighborhoods of cities North and South. But it wasn't until after World War I that the general public became aware of this powerful current in American music. The first authentic blues record—"Crazy Blues," sung by Mamie Smith—appeared in 1920 and started an avalanche. The twenties were to prove the golden age of vocal blues. Blues swept the country and saturated jazz through and through.

The first jazz instrumentalists followed the phrasing and even the breathing of the blues singers. Early horn players, most of whom couldn't read music and didn't know about the supposed limitations of their instruments, simply copied the inflections of vocal blues, sliding into notes and slurring or "bending" them to produce a blues effect.

Blues run all through jazz, through every period, style and school. Early New Orleans trumpet men—Buddy Bolden, King Oliver, Louis Armstrong—all played blues. Duke Ellington has written countless blues. The great bop innovator, Charlie Parker, wrote more blues than anything else. Today, all the great jazz figures play blues in one form or another. Whether their styles are called Dixieland, swing, bop, progressive, hard-bop, abstract, third stream, or simply far out, you can be sure they are all linked in the great family tradition of the blues.

Where did the blues get its name? The word "blues" to describe a mood was used in England in Elizabethan times. People spoke of "blue devils" when they felt down in the dumps. In this country, "blues" was a common term for boredom or unhappiness all through the nineteenth century. As early as 1807, Washington Irving was writing about the "blues," meaning a melancholy state of mind.

Leadbelly, the famous folk singer, described the mood of the blues this way:

> When you lay down at night, turn from one side of the bed all night to the other and can't sleep, what's the matter? Blues got you. Or when you get up in the morning and sit on the side of the bed—may have a mother or father, sister or brother, boy friend or girl friend, or husband or wife around—you don't want no talk out of 'em. They ain't done you nothin', you ain't done them nothin'—but what's the matter? Blues got you.

The music called the blues expressed, first of all, the troubles and confusions of American Negroes as they moved from slavery to freedom. The problems of the people who created these songs were very real. In the last quarter of the nineteenth century, the cotton kingdom of the South was crumbling, and with it the livelihood of great numbers of Negro farmworkers. Many ex-slaves, without training or special skills, became migrant laborers who drifted from one construction job to another—cutting timber, raising levees, building railroads. Others drifted to towns, where they huddled together in Negro ghettos. The jobs they found were those nobody else wanted—the menial or backbreaking jobs at the bottom of the economic ladder. They were paid low wages and were the first to be fired in bad times.

The blues tells the story of these years—of the Negroes' poverty, rootless wanderings, love troubles, homesickness, brushes with the law. It treats these woes with natural simplicity and honesty.

But there is another side to the blues. Negroes were used to facing disaster with stoicism. They had a great capacity for hope, rooted in the teachings of the Christian religion. They also were able to laugh at their troubles, to lighten the deepest gloom with shafts of ironic wit and humor. This bittersweet mood, the contrast of feeling, the unexpected laughter, gave the blues its great emotional appeal. Among the Negroes who invented them, blues acted as a safety valve for the feelings of both singer and audience. An example of a mournful blues with a quick recovery is this ancient standard:

> I'm goin' down to the railroad train and
>   lay my head on the track,
> I'm goin' down to the railroad train and
>   lay my head on the track,
> But if I see the train a-comin', I'm gonna
>   jerk it back.

The blues was always used as dance music. The early blues singer followed the harvests, turned up at farm towns when Negro workers had a few extra coins jingling in their pockets and sang and played his guitar for Saturday night dances. With his voice, his guitar, and his foot tapping out a steady beat, the country blues singer was a one-man dance band.

In spite of these good-time associations, blues are close to spirituals. "Minnie the Moocher" and "St. James Infirmary"—both low-down blues—are identical, except in lyrics, with the spiritual "Keep Your Hands on the Plow." A good example of a spiritual on the way to becoming a blues is "Lord, I Just Can't Keep from Crying" sung by Blind Willie Johnson (Jazz, Folkways, Vol. 2).

Blues singers and jazz musicians, themselves, often link blues and Negro religious music. Guitarist T-Bone Walker told an interviewer: "Of course the blues comes a lot from church. . . . The preacher used to preach in a bluesy tone sometimes." The great blues singer, Bessie Smith, recorded a number called "Preachin' the Blues."

Like spirituals, the blues is based on the holler—the "cry" which is the core sound of all American Negro folk music and, indeed, of jazz. The old-time blues shouter sang in holler style. He started each line strong and let his voice fall away to a low-pitched murmur or growl. Such blues were actually hollers, strung together with a regular rhythm on a simple chord base.

When slaves hollered in southern fields, they used "blue notes"—partly flattened notes that gave their songs a plaintive sound. They slurred the third and seventh notes of the scale in a way that can't be shown exactly on paper. They "worried" these notes, wavering between major and minor keys. Blue tonality is the result of adding these two blue notes to the ordinary scale.

Where did the blue notes come from? It seems probable

that these notes were used in West African singing and were brought here in colonial times by the slaves. Some writers think blue tonality may have started in India, traveled through the Arab countries and settled in Africa. There certainly seems to be an affinity between the blues and the music of mosque and synagogue.

But there's more to the blues than blue tonality. Not every sad slow song that uses blue notes is a blues. A real blues has a fixed structure as well defined as that of a sonnet in poetry or a fugue in classical music.

The basic blues formula calls for twelve bars of music divided into three four-bar lines. The melody is based on a series of simple chords—the same chords that can be found in any number of familiar hymns and folk songs, from "Silent Night" to "Yankee Doodle." This form proved marvelously adaptable in jazz. It was a framework which jazzmen could fill with endless variations.

The blues follows a definite pattern in its lyrics, too. The first line makes a statement; the second line repeats that statement; and the third line delivers the punch.

> If you see me comin', hoist your window high,
> If you see me comin', hoist your window high,
> And if you see me goin', hang your head and cry.

The words take up only a little more than half the length of each musical line. The rest of the space is filled in with a "break"—a short musical passage played by one or more instruments. Through this device, the blues carries on the call-and-response tradition of Negro folk music. The vocal part of each line is the call and corresponds to the part sung by the leader of a southern work gang or chanted by the minister in a country church. The "break" corresponds to the pause in which the workers sing a chorus in unison or the members of the church congregation burst out with, "Yes, Lord," or "Amen!"

Early blues shouters made up new verses as they went along. The break at the end of one line gave them time to think up another. They filled in these pauses by playing the guitar or banjo, or blowing on a harmonica. Later singers had the backing of piano, horn or full orchestra. The instrumental passages always had a close responsive relation to what had come before in the vocal parts.

The first man to write down and publish blues was William Christopher Handy. He started to put blues on paper around 1910 in Memphis. He didn't invent these blues, as he himself often pointed out; he based them on fragments of folk melody and earthy lyrics he had heard all his life. Handy was a talented composer, and he pieced these scraps together and shaped them into enduring blues classics—"St. Louis Blues," "Beale Street Blues," "Loveless Love," "Aunt Hagar's Blues" and many others. As the first musician to document this music, Handy started the blues on the road to world-wide fame.

Handy's eighty-five-year lifetime spanned a great stretch of jazz history. He was five years older than Buddy Bolden, the legendary pioneer of New Orleans jazz; yet he lived to see many of the revolutionary jazz developments of modern times.

Handy was born in 1873 in Florence, Alabama, in a log cabin with a dirt floor. His parents were former slaves—poor, respectable and highly religious. His father, who was a Methodist minister, disapproved of all worldly music and held dance music to be downright sinful. The only songs the boy heard at home were hymns.

In school, young Handy was taught to look down on the "primitive" music of slave days. He went to the Florence District School for Negroes, where a zealous singing teacher taught his pupils to read notes, to sing in all keys and to harmonize. The pupils in this school sang no spirituals, but they were introduced to the works of Wagner, Bizet and Verdi.

Handy liked the music lessons in his school, but he was even more drawn to the strains of folk music that he heard all about him. The hollers of Negro plowmen, who worked in nearby fields, floated through the open windows of his classroom. He heard their plaintive cries:

> A-o-oo-a-o,
> I wouldn't live in Cairo,
> A-o-oo, A-o-oo . . .

He worked as a water boy at a stone quarry when he was twelve years old and there heard Negro steel drivers shout out rhythmical work songs. As they swung their hammers in unison, the men sang:

> Oh baby, 'member last winter,
> Wasn't it cold—*huh?*
> Wasn't it cold—*huh?*

The *huh*'s were grunts of exhaled breath that burst from the workers as their hammers drove steel spikes deep into the rock.

He also heard Negro boys playing homemade musical instruments on the streets—drawing a nail across the teeth of a jawbone of a horse for rhythmic effects, singing through paper-wrapped combs, and beating on tin pans and milk pails. These street-corner combos were training schools for future jazzmen.

Young Handy worked at many jobs as he was growing up —at plastering, shoemaking, carpentry. He picked cotton and worked as a janitor. He gave most of his earnings to his family; but he also saved for a guitar.

When he was at last able to buy the guitar, his joy in its

possession was short-lived. His father called it a "devil's play-thing" and made the boy exchange it for a dictionary.

Handy's next musical purchase was a battered cornet, which he bought secretly for $1.75 and kept in school. He practiced fingering at his desk and eventually became skilled enough to play with a Florence band. When he was fifteen, he joined a traveling minstrel show in spite of his parents' strong objections; and he began a roaming life that brought him into contact with the folk sources of the blues.

He knew hard times when shows folded and the players were stranded. He slept in vacant lots, on levees and slumped on chairs in poolrooms. He worked between minstrel jobs at any kind of manual labor—anything to keep from going home to a chorus of "I told you so's."

All through these years, Handy heard and filed away for future reference fragments of song that expressed the deepest feelings of the poor people among whom he lived. These were the songs of sadness, loneliness, protest and stoical humor out of which he would later weave his blues.

He once heard a washer-woman singing as she pinned a man's shirt to a line of flapping clothes: "Your clothes look lonesome hanging on the line. . . ." He was moved by the plaintive words, half-sung, half-chanted, that arranged themselves into a perfect blues line. Years later, Handy remembered this strange scrap of song and used it in "Aunt Hagar's Blues," a piece he dashed off in a Chicago barbershop.

In Tennessee, he heard a song about Joe Turner, a white man in charge of taking Negro prisoners to the penitentiary at Nashville. Turner had many Negroes arrested on trumped-up charges, so the story went, to get convict labor for farms in that area. If anyone asked what became of these men, the answer was, "They tell me Joe Turner's come and gone." Negro women in Tennessee sang:

He come wid forty links of chain, Oh Lawdy!
Come wid forty links of chain, Oh Lawdy!
Got my man and gone.

Handy heard this song, with words changed to suit local conditions, throughout the South. It inspired his own "Joe Turner Blues."

In 1896, Handy joined Mahara's Minstrels, one of the top Negro minstrel troupes of the day. He first played bass violin in the orchestra, then trumpet. Soon he was training vocal groups in the company and arranging accompaniments for the featured singers. After the first season, he was promoted to leader of the forty-two musicians in the band. He traveled from Cuba to California, and from Canada to Mexico, playing to white as well as Negro audiences. Mahara's had the pick of talented musicians of that day. They offered semi-classical music, sentimental ballads, marches, ragtime, and old plantation tunes—a mixture that would one day blend into jazz.

Handy left Mahara's Minstrels to settle down to direct a band in Clarksdale, Mississippi. Handy said later that he was drawn to Mississippi by the blues. The delta country was the heart of blues territory.

Once when Handy sat waiting for a train in the railroad station of a small town in Mississippi, he heard a ragged Negro street singer plucking a guitar. The singer sang a mournful tune. He kept repeating one line: "Goin' where the Southern cross the Dog." He was singing about two railroad lines, the Great Southern and the Yazoo Delta, nicknamed "Yellow Dog" by the Negroes who worked on its construction. These lines crossed near a Negro penitentiary. Perhaps the singer sang out of sorrowful personal knowledge of this prison. At any rate, his song gave Handy the theme for his "Yellow Dog Blues."

Handy wrote in his autobiography, *Father of the Blues*, that the turning point in his musical life occurred at a Negro dance in Cleveland, Mississippi, in 1903. Handy and his band played conventional dance numbers; but the dancers wanted what one of them called "our native music." A local group took the stand with a battered guitar, a mandolin, and a worn-out string bass. These players, Handy ruefully admitted, had the stuff the people wanted. They played a plaintive strain that sprang from cane rows and levee camps, repeating the simple tune over and over and stamping out a powerful beat with their feet. The dancers went wild and showered the ragged musicians with coins.

The country band had taught Handy something not in books. He went back to Clarksdale and started to orchestrate folk tunes he had heard all his life, like "Make Me a Pallet on the Floor." His band became much more popular, and they played for many social and political events.

Handy's first blues was written for a mayoralty campaign in Memphis, Tennessee. His band was hired by one of the candidates to entertain the voters. After the campaign, Handy changed the lyrics and published the piece himself as the "Memphis Blues." Handy in time became a canny business man, but he sold away the rights to his first blues for fifty dollars.

"Memphis Blues" uses the classic twelve-bar, three-line blues form. Handy used flatted third and seventh notes of the scale to suggest the slurred blue notes of Negro folk music. This piece, too, contained a written "break"—probably the first in jazz history.

The most famous of all Handy blues, "The St. Louis Blues," was written in 1914. His inspiration came from a fragment of speech he overheard on the street, "My man's got a heart like a rock cast in the sea. . . ." The line sang itself in a slow mournful blues tune in Handy's head.

Handy wrote the "St. Louis Blues" in one night. The tango was in style then, and he decided to use a tango rhythm for the beginning and middle sections of his piece. This accounts for the "Spanish tinge" of this great blues. Handy said he "tricked" the dancers by the tango introduction before breaking into low-down blues.

The "St. Louis Blues" was a great success, and Handy followed it with "Yellow Dog Blues," "Hesitating Blues," and "Beale Street Blues." All of these compositions were built around or suggested by folk tunes, snatches of songs and old blues. The richness and vitality of his music came from these deep folk sources.

Handy saw blues become thoroughly respectable. They invaded concert halls and opera stages. Paul Whiteman, who was intent on "making a lady out of jazz," presented George Gershwin's "Rhapsody in Blue" in Aeolian Hall in New York City in 1924 with full symphonic flourish.

Handy had his ups and downs, his periods of prosperity and recognition, and other times when he was seemingly forgotten by the public. By the early forties, an eye ailment that had long troubled him worsened, and he became totally blind. Handy's thoughts in affliction turned to old Negro songs of hope and courage. He decided, in his own words, to "wear the world as a loose garment" and to keep a "rainbow 'round my shoulder."

In spite of his blindness, Handy was able to resume an active productive life. He lived to see his blues go around the world. He ran his own music publishing business until a few months before his death in 1958 and was energetic and cheerful to the last.

One milestone in his later life was a 1954 recording session that produced "Louis Armstrong Plays W. C. Handy" (Columbia CL 591). Handy sat in the studio while Armstrong taped a superb performance of Handy classics. Tears streamed from the old gentleman's sightless eyes and he exclaimed, "Truly wonderful! Truly wonderful! Nobody could have done it but my boy Louis!"

The blues tradition is as strong among modern jazz composers as it was a half-century ago, when Handy wrote the numbers Armstrong sang at this session. Jazz composers and performers of the present are true to the blues form even when they transform it—as Charlie Parker did—with dazzling runs of sixteenth notes, with advanced harmonic effects, and with the most subtle rhythmic variations.

The blues is still a vital vibrant music of intense communicative power. Miles Davis, Gerry Mulligan, Jimmy Giuffre and Dizzy Gillespie are just a few of the fine interpreters of the blues among modern jazzmen. Behind them stretches a long line of blues artists, known and unknown, who gave the blues its unique form and sound.

CHAPTER SIX

BLUES SINGERS

Bessie Smith and Others

Blind Lemon Jefferson is typical of the primitive country blues singers who roamed the South in the early part of this century. His songs show clearly the transition from Negro folk music to out-and-out blues. He recast old field hollers and work songs into blues and sang them in a high, hard, "crying" voice—a style favored by Texas men. There were many other good blues shouters around at that time; but Lemon happened to make many recordings, and he's the best known.

Lemon was born in 1897 in Central Texas, the son of a poor farmer. He was born blind and knew from early childhood that music was his only hope for escape from a life of dependence and bitter poverty. He soaked up the mournful tunes he heard at home and in the fields, the driving chanting and hand-clapping of church services, the rocking beat of Negro good-time music. He taught himself to play the guitar. By the time he was in his teens, he was singing and playing for pennies on the streets of towns near his home.

In 1917, Lemon went to Dallas to try his luck. He was a

fat country boy, too proud to admit that he was blind or to let anybody lead him. He didn't know a soul in Dallas and almost starved before he became established among the Negroes in the city's slums. He made up a blues about his hardships:

> I stood on a corner and almost bust my head,
> I couldn't earn enough money to buy me a
>   loaf of bread.

The Negro section of Dallas in those days had an intense musical life. It was a stopping-off place for musicians from all parts of the country. Lemon learned from everybody. He had a prodigious memory for songs, and he was a tireless performer. By the early twenties he was an established entertainer, no longer worried about where his next meal was coming from.

Lemon became famous over a wide circuit of southern towns. He was constantly on the go in cotton-picking time, playing wherever there were crowds of Negroes with money jingling in their pockets. He sat on a stool and played on busy street corners, a wide-brimmed Stetson hat shading his face from the broiling sun. He was by then enormously fat, and his guitar rode high on his great paunch. At night, he played and sang at dances.

By 1926, Lemon was in Chicago, putting on records his hard plaintive blues. He recorded eighty-one blues in all, over a four-year period. By the time he died in 1930, his singing style had lost much of its old time back-country flavor. He died tragically, frozen to death when he tried to grope his way alone through a Chicago snowstorm.

William (Big Bill) Broonzy started in the same blues shouting tradition as Blind Lemon; but in his forty-year career, he was able to transform his songs into a more moving and subtle kind of communication, without losing the elemental folk quality.

Broonzy was born on a farm in Mississippi in 1893, one of seventeen children. His mother had been born in slavery, and he learned the old songs of the Negro past from her and from the poor country people among whom he was raised. The church was a strong influence. As Big Bill said in "The Bill Broonzy Story," recorded by Verve near the end of his life, "Every blues singer I know sung spirituals before he sung the blues. . . ."

Broonzy loved the blues. He was fascinated by all the stories that could be told in blues form. "Now you can take a chair, a box, an ax, a knife—anything—and you can start writing a blues from it." As a young man Bill roamed the country working as a farm hand, miner, preacher, janitor and piano mover. He composed blues to fit these occupations—"Plough Hand Blues," "Moppin' Blues," and so forth. He tried to make an easier life for himself as a professional entertainer, but he usually had to hold other jobs as well.

Broonzy was a forceful singer, a master of timing and accent, and he used his guitar as an expressive second voice. He was more lyrical than most country blues singers, and he had a fine sense of irony. Like Leadbelly, with whom he once worked on a railroad section gang, Big Bill was able to build an intense communication between himself and an audience. He said, "Maybe the blues will die some day, but I'll have to die first."

Broonzy wrote over three hundred songs during his lifetime and made many recordings. He generally stayed close to the basic twelve-bar form and simple chord structure of early blues. He once wrote a song that began with an old cry heard on southern levees, "Oh I feel like hollering, but the town is too small. . . ." Bill resisted any pressure to make his style slicker and more commercial. As he explained, "For me to really sing the old blues that I learned in Mississippi I have to go back to my sound and not the right chords as the musicians have told me to make. The real blues is played and sung the way you feel. . . ."

Some audiences thought Broonzy's songs were old-fashioned, although fellow musicians, including Duke Ellington and Count Basie, understood and appreciated what he was trying to do. After World War II, Big Bill found it so hard to earn a living with his kind of blues that he took a job as janitor at Iowa State College. Happily, there was a resurgence of interest in blues as an "art form" in the fifties, and Bill had a few good years touring in this country and Europe before he died.

One July night in 1957, Broonzy spent ten hours in a recording studio putting his story on tape. The result was "The Bill Broonzy Story" (Verve V-3000-5), an extraordinarily rich musical and social documentary. In these five LP's, Broonzy told in his own words and songs the history of the blues, from the old work songs and spirituals to rock-and-roll.

Big Bill died at the age of sixty-five, a month after this recording session. He left behind him an honest and beautiful record of the blues and of the feeling and experiences that produced them.

One of the great living blues singers is Jimmy Rushing, the original "Mister Five by Five." Like many other blues performers, Jimmy comes from the Southwest. He was born and raised in Oklahoma City in a highly musical family. An uncle from the Deep South taught Jimmy his first blues and told him, "The blues means twelve bars."

Jimmy started singing professionally in California night spots, later joined Count Basie in Kansas City and was a mainstay of the Basie organization for fifteen years.

Rushing combines the vigor of an old-time blues shouter

with a sensitive and melodic personal style. Like Broonzy, he is an eloquent spokesman for the blues. He traces blues to spirituals, "he-and-she songs," and work songs of slave days. "Today, as it was then," he explains, "the blues comes right back to a person's feelings, to his daily activities in life. But rich people don't know nothing about the blues, please believe me."

Jimmy shows his ties to the past in many ways. He often ends a blues according to an old tradition: "Anybody ask you who was it sang this song, tell 'em little Jimmy Rushing, he's been here and gone." Jimmy's memories of a lifetime of singing the blues are summed up in a musical journey to New Orleans, Kansas City, Chicago and New York in "The Jazz Odyssey of James Rushing, Esq.," (Columbia CL 963).

Texas produced Jack Teagarden, a big burly trombonist and vocalist, who sings a soft, slurred, relaxed blues. When Teagarden arrived in New York in 1927, he was known as the only white musician who could sing the blues in an "authentic" manner. Jack cut a vocal side in 1929 that was based on an ancient blues:

> I'd rather drink muddy water, Lawd, sleep in a
>   hollow log,
> Than to be away up here in New York, treated
>   like a dirty dog.

Teagarden has teamed up with many notable jazz musicians, but he is best known for his amiable duets with Louis Armstrong. He trouped all over the world with Armstrong—his burry baritone a fine foil for Louis' rasps and growls.

Ray Charles is probably the best male blues singer around. Charles, who has been blind since childhood, is a singer, pianist, organist and saxophonist. He sings blues with the contagious beat and hot shouting tone of an old-time Negro sermon. Charles has managed to please both sophisticated jazz critics and the rock-and-roll trade—no mean feat. His records are runaway best sellers. "It's All Right" (Atlantic 8025) is a good sample.

Women became professional blues singers later than men; but they made the first blues records and became much better known than their male predecessors. Women created a buoyant sassy kind of blues devoted almost exclusively to the "he-and-she" theme. Theirs were "city" blues, smoother and more melodic than the "country" songs of the male blues shouters, but with the same folk roots.

The first of the great line of women blues singers was Gertrude (Ma) Rainey. She was born in Columbus, Georgia, in 1886, the daughter of Negro show people. At fifteen, she married Will Rainey and went on the road with his troupe, the Rabbit Foot Minstrels. According to her own account, Ma first heard blues in 1902 and sang them from then on. She toured for years in minstrels, tent shows, and on the T.O.B.A. (Theatre Owners' Booking Association), which was the Negro vaudeville circuit. Her name became a household word among Negroes of the South and Midwest.

She discovered Bessie Smith in Tennessee when Bessie was a young girl and helped and encouraged her.

Ma was a short heavy woman, famous for her good humor. In one historic performance in New Orleans, she was singing a blues that went: "If you don't believe I'm sinkin', look what a hole I'm in. . . ." Just as she reached the words, "look what a hole I'm in," the stage collapsed—but Ma went right on singing.

Ma recorded during the twenties. She made about a hundred sides on the Paramount label for the Negro trade. These sides are marred by surface noises, for Paramount used a primitive recording process. Her records do not compare technically to those made at another studio at the same time by Bessie Smith. Nevertheless, Ma's dignity and power, and the harsh-edged richness of her voice come through even the rough recordings that she left to us. Original Rainey records are now collectors' items. Some good examples are reproduced in the Folkways Jazz series, Volumes 2, 4 and 11.

The roster of musicians who accompanied Ma in her recording dates reads like a who's-who of jazz immortals. Louis Armstrong backed her with infinitely lyrical, tender trumpet passages, phrased exactly as though he, too, were singing the blues. Buster Bailey on clarinet, Charlie Green on trombone, Fletcher Henderson on piano—these were a few of the legendary jazzmen who supplied the responses to Ma's blues.

Ma Rainey retired in 1933 and settled in Rome, Georgia. She lived there peacefully until her death in 1939.

Her pupil, Bessie Smith, had a much more turbulent career. Bessie was probably the best blues singer of all time.

There's a story that when the great cornet player, Bix Beiderbecke, heard Bessie Smith at the Paradise Gardens in Chicago, he threw a whole week's pay on the floor to keep her singing. The legends about Bessie are legion. True or not, they convey the aura of greatness and enchantment that once surrounded this woman—who, more than anybody else, seemed born to sing the blues.

Bessie Smith was called the "Queen of the Blues" by Negro audiences and "Empress of the Blues" by her record company. She was a big majestic woman who stood five-feet-nine inches tall and weighed over two hundred pounds. She had a beautiful round, bronze-colored face, and she liked to wear big earrings and regal headdresses. She had a voice to match her stature, a full rich contralto of seemingly limitless power. When microphones appeared, Bessie Smith pushed them away.

Bessie was a mistress of blue inflection. She could hit notes straight or "bend" them. She could phrase lyrics to wring

every shade of meaning and feeling out of them. She drew
on the old, deep, country sources of the blues.

At the height of her career, from about 1923 to 1927,
Bessie was a great popular idol. She traveled with her own
show and earned up to $1500 a week—a fabulous salary for
a Negro artist in those days. Her records sold in the millions. Negroes stood in long lines at record shops to buy the
latest Bessie Smith recordings.

Bessie sang one sad blues called the "Long Old Road." The
long road she traveled began in Chattanooga, Tennessee,
where she was born about 1894. She was one of five children
brought up in grim poverty. While she was still in her teens,
she was taken under Ma Rainey's wing. Ma was visiting
Chattanooga with the Rabbit Foot Minstrels, heard young
Bessie sing, and decided to take her with the show.

Bessie was influenced by Ma Rainey's direct earthy approach to the blues. She learned to anticipate or retard the
beat, to underline a phrase with a slow broad vibrato, to slide
from note to note for blue-toned effect. But Bessie was capable
of a greater range—vocal and emotional—than Ma. The pupil
soon outshone the teacher.

Bessie toured with tent shows and carnivals through the
rural South for a few years. She gradually worked up to being
a star on the Negro vaudeville circuit.

When Bessie sang, she would walk slowly to the center of
the stage to the accompaniment of muted brasses and pounding drums. Then she would plant her monumental frame
solidly in the center of the stage, throw her head back, and
let the blues roll out—very simply, without any distracting
mannerisms or movement.

Danny Barker, a New Orleans guitarist, says in his vivid
recollections of Bessie in Shapiro and Hentoff's *Hear Me
Talkin' to Ya:*

Bessie was a fabulous deal to watch. She was a pretty large woman and she could sing the blues. . . . You didn't turn your head when she went on. You just watched Bessie. . . . She just upset you. . . . If you had any church background, like people who came from the South as I did, you would recognize a similarity between what she was doing and what those preachers and evangelists from there did. . . . She could bring about mass hypnotism. When she was performing, you could hear a pin drop.

Bessie appeared in a film in 1929, a Warner Brothers short called *St. Louis Blues*. The film itself is a tasteless caricature of Negro life; but Bessie's majestic physical presence and the deep feeling with which she infuses her role transcend the shoddy script. To hear Bessie sing Handy's blues classic in the film is a spine-tingling experience. The sound track of this solo has been transcribed on records. It can be heard in "Great Blues Singers" (Riverside RLP 12-121).

Bessie recorded many blues over a ten-year period beginning in 1923, and her accompanists include some of the greatest names in jazz.

A white man, Frank Walker, "discovered" Bessie for the Columbia Record Company. He first heard her sing in a cabaret in Selma, Alabama. He later recalled, "I never heard anything like the torture and torment she put into the music of her people. It was the blues, and she meant it." When Walker, who was director of recording for Columbia, decided to release some real blues, instead of watered-down imitations, he remembered Bessie and brought her to New York.

Her first record was "Down Hearted Blues," which sold a million copies, mostly to Negroes. In spite of the title, this song had a joyous twist; Bessie sang, "got the world in a jug, got the stopper in my hand." On later records, she sang about the sorrows of the poor, the friendless, the betrayed. She sang "I love you baby, but I can't stand mistreatment no more," and "I hate a man that don't play fair and square"; and her listeners felt understood and helped in their troubles.

One of Bessie's greatest recordings was "Back Water Blues" about a great Mississippi flood.

> When it rained five days and the sky
>   turned black at night,
> When it thundered and lightnin'ed and
>   the wind began to blow,
> Back water blues done caused me to pack
>   my things and go,
> 'Cause my house fell down and I can't
>   live there no more.

Bessie was backed in this number by James P. Johnson, who was a composer and arranger as well as the dean of Harlem pianists. Johnson had the knack of underlining Bessie's lyrics and paraphrasing her way of singing in the piano passages. There was no rehearsing for Bessie's record dates. She and her accompanist simply improvised on the basic blues line— inspiring each other as they went along. Bessie made up many of the lyrics herself.

Bessie recorded exclusively for Columbia. Frank Walker was an honest and conscientious adviser. He tried hard to make Bessie put aside some of her earnings, and he made her buy a house for her own use in Philadelphia. But Bessie liked to live high, to throw her money around and to treat the drifters and spongers who attached themselves to her. At one time, she bought a boarding house where her friends could live free.

Bessie liked noise and excitement. She liked to have the center of the spotlight onstage and off. She could be rough and tough—but she also could be gentle and sympathetic. At the height of her career, she once canceled three weeks of bookings to help the Walkers when their young son was seriously ill. She cooked and cleaned for the family so that Mrs. Walker would be free to take care of the sick child.

By 1930, Bessie's career was on the downgrade. The Depression had hit the country with a disastrous effect on the recording industry. People listened to their radios instead of buying phonograph records. At the same time, the tastes of the Negro public were changing. Fewer people wanted to hear the old-time blues that were Bessie's stock in trade. She tried to change with the times with little success.

Bessie had to go back to barnstorming—doing one-night stands, losing sleep and traveling long distances to fill engagements. She became surly and difficult. Her voice grew rougher and harsher. She was spending money as lavishly as ever, and she took any kind of work—even doing mammy routines in costume—to earn money.

Her last recording date was in 1933. It was arranged by Frank Walker and John Hammond, a jazz authority who has helped many artists in the field. Bessie was in a rollicking mood for this session, which produced, among other numbers, "Gimme a Pigfoot," a song in blues style about the custom of handing out free pigs-feet at New Orleans saloons. Her voice on this record was better than it had been for several years, and Walker and Hammond hoped that Bessie was back on the right track.

But the market for Bessie's records had almost disappeared. Ironically, as she lost her hold on the Negro public, she was discovered by white students of jazz and folk music. In 1936, she appeared at a Sunday afternoon jam session in New York sponsored by the United Hot Clubs of America. Bessie didn't even take off her cheap furs as she sang a few songs, and she returned immediately to the hit-and-miss jobs she was forced to play for a living.

The following year, Bessie was fatally injured in an automobile accident that occurred as she was being rushed from one such job to another. The car in which she was riding collided with a parked truck near the town of Clarksdale, Mississippi. Bessie was badly hurt. Whether or not she could have been saved if she had been admitted promptly to a nearby white hospital is still a matter of bitter debate.

John Hammond wrote this eulogy of Bessie shortly after her death:

> To my way of thinking, Bessie Smith was the greatest artist American jazz ever produced. In fact, I'm not sure that her art did not reach beyond the limits of the term 'jazz.' She was one of those rare beings, a completely integrated artist capable of projecting her whole personality into music. . . .

Bessie's recording career has been summed up in a superb set of four disks, "The Bessie Smith Story" (Columbia CL 855-858).

There were other notable women blues singers in Ma Rainey's and Bessie Smith's era. One of the most beautiful blues recordings of all time was made by Bertha (Chippie) Hill and Louis Armstrong in 1925 (Jazz, Vol. 4, Folkways FJ 1803). Chippie sang "Trouble in Mind" in a smooth, sad, sweet young woman's voice, and Armstrong backed her with some of the most moving trumpet passages in all jazz.

Another fine blues singer who made a splash in the twenties and then dropped from sight for many years is Ida Cox. Ida lacked Bessie Smith's power, but she was considered a great interpreter of the folk poetry of the blues. Like many other early blues singers, Ida turned to church singing. She was found recently living quietly in her old birthplace, Knoxville, Tennessee, and induced to come to New York to record an album for Riverside. The result was "Blues for Rampart Street" (Riverside 9374), her first recording in twenty-two years.

Many of the best known women vocalists in the jazz and popular fields have strong ties to the blues, even when they are not primarily blues singers. The late Billie Holiday was deeply influenced by records of Bessie Smith she heard as a child. Mildred Bailey gave popular songs a lovely, haunting blues inflection. Ivie Anderson, featured vocalist with Duke Ellington for eleven years, put many of the Duke's brand of blues on records.

Among present-day singers, Ella Fitzgerald is famous for her lovely, lilting treatment of show tunes and ballads; her blues background gives just a hint of blues expressiveness to these songs. Dinah Washington made some excellent blues recordings in the forties but leans more, nowadays, to pop material. Other sometimes-blues-singers who can be heard on rock-and-roll programs include La Vern Baker and Ruth Brown.

Real blues are seldom sung today. Long ago, a major shift from vocal to instrumental blues took place, and the jazz orchestra became the important creative force in the blues field. New Orleans was one of the historic spots where blues singers and future jazz musicians met, with lasting effect on our music.

André Hodeir, the brilliant French jazz critic, feels that "the clash of blues and military marches" in New Orleans was a high point in jazz history, "transforming an almost motionless folklore into an art capable of all kinds of evolution."

CHAPTER SEVEN

NEW ORLEANS

Musical Melting Pot

Much has been written to debunk the legend that New Orleans was the birthplace of jazz. Jazz was, indeed, sprouting up all over at the beginning of this century. Minstrel tunes, ragtime and blues were changing the shape of American music from coast to coast. New Orleans simply happened to furnish a remarkably fertile seedbed for jazz. The new music (it wasn't to be called "jazz" until about 1917) flourished there as nowhere else during its earliest years.

New Orleans was a gay and cosmopolitan city when its great jazz musicians were growing up. Its people were of every nationality, hue and accent, but the dominant culture was French. The French were the first settlers of New Orleans, and they tried to keep their city close in spirit to Paris. They cultivated the arts and a graceful leisurely way of life. They had a French Opera House before the Civil War; they followed the French craze for brass bands; they spoke a French Creole dialect; and they ate French food with a dash of Spanish seasoning. The Spaniards, too, had their turn at ruling New Orleans and left their mark on the city, especially on the style of architecture—houses with lacy iron grillwork on the outside and hidden courtyards and patios within.

The large Negro population of New Orleans was drawn mainly from two sources: from plantations around the city where Negro folk music still had a strongly African character, and from islands in the Caribbean where African traditions were also well preserved. These Negroes had lived in Latin-Catholic cultures that permitted them considerable leeway in matters of religion. French and Spanish planters didn't try to Christianize their slaves as vigorously as English-Protestant owners did. Even when these Negroes became Catholic, strong traces of their ancestral beliefs survived. In old New Orleans, as in Haiti today, Catholic saints and voodoo deities often shared the same altars.

Voodoo was originally a West African religion in which many spirits, both good and evil, were thought to play a magical role in human affairs. In voodoo rites, the worshippers use powerful drum rhythms and tirelessly repeated chanting and dancing to bring about a trance state in which they are "possessed" by these spirits. Many of the Negroes of New Orleans came from tribes that practiced voodoo. New Orleans became the voodoo capital of the United States, and an empty lot known as Congo Square became the center for voodoo dances.

These dances flourished between 1817 and 1885 and had a strong influence on the formation of New Orleans jazz. They kept alive complicated African rhythms that had all but disappeared elsewhere in this country. Drummers from the West Indies played several different kinds of drums in Congo Square —including the bamboula, a hollow tube of bamboo with sheepskin stretched across one end. Others shook gourds, jingled bells, and rattled animal jawbones that had been dried in the sun until the teeth were loosened. Negro dancers and spectators clapped and stamped, and sang in a French-African dialect that was unintelligible to white tourists who flocked to the square.

Buddy Bolden, the first great Negro cornetist of New Orleans jazz, was in his teens when these gatherings ended. King Oliver and Louis Armstrong were born too late to hear the drums of Congo Square, but voodoo rhythms were still enmeshed in the songs and dances of New Orleans Negroes in their day.

A second important influence on New Orleans jazz was the prevalence of military bands. The citizens of the city were band-mad. No social, political or sports event was complete without the presence of a brass band in full uniform.

Before the Civil War, these bands employed only white musicians or colored Creoles of mixed African, French and Spanish ancestry. After the war, musicians of purely Negro stock formed their own bands.

New Orleans Negroes had many clubs devoted to pleasure and social aid. These clubs had large dues-paying memberships and bore fanciful or boastful names, such as the "Hobgoblins," the "Zulus," the "Money Wasters" and the "Diamond Swells." When these clubs paraded—which they did often— they marched to the music of their own brass bands. This custom created jobs for many Negro musicians, and rivalries between clubs spurred them to great heights of musical invention.

The Negro funeral parades of New Orleans are famous in jazz history. The custom was to march slowly to the cemetery with a band playing solemn hymns, such as "Rock of Ages" and "Nearer My God to Thee." But on the return trip from the cemetery, the band launched into lively syncopated tunes, such as "High Society" or "Panama." As Jelly Roll Morton, the celebrated New Orleans pianist, put it: ". . . 'Rejoice unto death' and 'Cry at the birth.' New Orleans stick close to that scripture. . . ."

A ragged line of children and assorted stragglers always followed these parades, strutting and dancing in the wake of the bands. This was the famous "second line" in which many a New Orleans jazzman got his musical education. Louis Armstrong mastered his first instrument—a tin whistle—in the second line.

Negro bands also worked at picnics, boat excursions and dances. They rode through the streets in large horse-drawn wagons to advertise these events in advance. Usually, five men rode on a wagon. The trombonist sat at the rear with the tailgate of the wagon lowered so that he would have plenty of room to work the slide. Connoisseurs of New Orleans jazz still speak of "tailgate trombone."

The real excitement began when the wagons of two rival bands met in the street and staged what was called a "cutting contest." Each band took a turn playing a favorite number and tried to best its adversary in musical skill, invention and sheer lung power. People came swarming from blocks around and picked the winner by applause. It was customary for the audience to fall in behind the winning band when it went on its triumphant way.

The high point of the year in New Orleans, for whites and Negroes alike, came with the celebration of Mardi Gras—a ten-day carnival with music that preceded Lent. All the usual gaiety of the city was heightened at this season with a series of spectacular parades and parties.

The Negro parade was a satire on the hoity-toity doings of the whites. King Zulu and his court rambled through the streets on a large float and tossed coconuts to their admirers. The Negro bands of the city marched with them.

All quarters joined in the Mardi Gras fun—including Storyville, a thirty-eight block district that overflowed with saloons, cabarets, dance halls and gambling dens. This district flourished all year around and kept a dozen dance bands and many solo pianists working every night. During its early history, only white musicians or light-skinned mulattoes worked in Storyville; but as the fame of Negro jazzmen grew, they, too, found jobs there. Storyville played an important role as the meeting ground for these different groups of musicians, all of whom influenced each other. In 1917, after many brawls and murders, this district finally shut down, and many of the jazzmen who had played there began drifting northward in search of new jobs.

It's a mistake to think that all early jazz was nurtured in Storyville. Some of New Orleans' most celebrated jazzmen, including Buddy Bolden, never worked there.

Charles (Buddy) Bolden is one of the legendary figures of jazz. He is reputed to have played one of the most powerful horns of all time. One veteran New Orleans jazzman said Bolden played his cornet louder than Louis Armstrong with the microphone turned on. Jelly Roll Morton called him "the blowingest man ever lived since Gabriel."

It's hard to say whether Bolden's fame rests on musicianship or on strong lungs and a supercharged personality. In his day he was undisputed king of the Negro musicians of New Orleans. He was so popular that he had six or seven bands going at the same time and went from one to another playing his specialties. Bolden was born in 1868 in a rough uptown neighborhood where the poorest Negroes of the city lived. His training school was the churning musical atmosphere of the Negro slums—in which voodoo ceremonies, shouting church services, military marches and primitive blues all flourished. He had no formal music lessons and, in fact, never learned to read notes, but he taught himself to play the cornet.

In those days, playing a musical instrument seemed to poor Negro boys in New Orleans a sure passport to fame and fortune. Outstanding band players were treated with the kind of adulation given to baseball stars today. Horns were favorite instruments, both because they were easy to carry in parades and easy to obtain. New Orleans pawnshops were flooded with the horns of army bandsmen at the end of the Civil War. They could be bought for a few dollars and were passed from musician to musician.

As a young man, Bolden ran a barbershop and published a gossip sheet called *The Cricket*. He also organized a dance band that met in the backroom of the barbershop. There was nothing unusual about a musician holding down several jobs. Many a New Orleans jazzman was a bricklayer, a cigar maker, or plasterer on the side.

Buddy's band included his cornet, and a trombone, clarinet, guitar, string bass and drums. This was the standard New Orleans line-up. A second cornet was added from time to time. (It should be noted that no pianos were used in New Orleans bands for the obvious reason that a piano can't be carried in a parade. Saxophones had already been invented but were not used at all in early jazz.)

At first Buddy was nicknamed "Kid," but as his fame grew, he became "King," the first New Orleans musician to win this title. Bolden had what is called nowadays "star quality." He generated excitement. Like Bessie Smith and Louis Armstrong, who came after him, he knew how to dominate an audience. When he raised his cornet to call his children home, as he called it, the Negroes of New Orleans flocked to him like the children of Hamelin to the Pied Piper.

King Bolden's men played the usual repertory of New Orleans bands—marches, ragtime, quadrilles and polkas. But what brought this group into the jazz orbit was the blues. Bolden's blues were much slower than those played today. He liked to play "Careless Love" and really moan it out. He could play Scott Joplin's "Maple Leaf Rag," when someone else read the music for him, but he preferred to play mean low-down blues. He liked to play for dancing and to hear the shuffling feet of dancers as a background to his music.

Most of the men in Bolden's band, like their leader, couldn't read music. Bolden usually kept one note-reader on the payroll to run through new pieces. The non-readers, who were called "fakers," would take it up from there.

"Faking" was a great spur to jazz in its earliest stages. Musicians who couldn't read were forced to improvise, to change the shape of written marches and ragtime pieces with new rhythms and flourishes. They naturally fell back on the blues and the older traditions of Negro folk singing.

In New Orleans bands, the cornet led the way, playing the basic melodic line and emphasizing the strong beats. The trombone supported the cornet, accenting the rhythm with huffs and puffs, and filling in the bottom of the design with low smears and growls. The clarinet took the part of the female voice. They improvised together like the members of a Negro church congregation singing a spiritual. The cornet was the song leader urging the flock along, while the trombone and clarinet wove their separate melodic lines into the basic text. This was the polyphonic structure of New Orleans jazz—the development of three separate and distinct strands of melody, played together with great artistry. In the background the bass, guitar and drums simply kept the rhythm going.

Bolden was always ready to drop his barber's scissors at a moment's notice to play at a neighborhood dance. He would stand in the doorway of a dance hall in the evening and play a few numbers to let the people know a dance was about to begin. All the windows for blocks around would be thrown open, and the kids would dance in the streets. Louis Armstrong was one of the small boys who came running when the King blew.

When Bolden played for a dance, he saved the meanest

blues for the last. About midnight, he would play "Don't Go Away Nobody," which was the signal for respectable people to leave. Then the band would break loose and the dancing became really rough. He always ended the night with a number called "Get Out of Here and Go Home."

On Sundays Bolden played in Johnson Park on the outskirts of the city. If the crowd happened to be listening to a rival who played in nearby Lincoln Park, Bolden would remark, "It's time to call my children home," and blow a mighty blast on his cornet. Jelly Roll Morton claimed, perhaps with the exaggeration due a legend, that the sound of Bolden's horn could be heard in the center of town, ten or twelve miles away.

Bolden also played at an outdoor dancing pavilion, at picnics and in street parades. It was customary in those days for a musician's best girl to march along with him in a parade and carry his musical instrument. Bolden was a great ladies' man, and he often marched with three girls—one to carry his cornet, the second his coat, and the third his hat.

Buddy's music, according to some jazz historians, was too "barrel-house" for refined tastes. A barrel-house was a low kind of drinking place—a rough, tough saloon with barrels of cheap whiskey lined up against one wall. An unrestrained kind of music played in these dives took on the name "barrelhouse." Another term for this music was "gut-bucket," which referred to the bucket that caught drippings or "gutterings" from the barrels. Both terms are still used.

Bolden reigned as undisputed champion of the uptown horn blowers until 1907, when he began to have dark and sometimes irrational moods. Perhaps years of hard living and overwork had something to do with it; at any rate, he ran amok during a Labor Day parade and had to be committed to a state asylum. He never recovered and finished out his life in this institution.

We have no records of Bolden's music, for he played before the days of modern recording. It is barely possible that he recorded on old Edison cylinders, but none have been unearthed. His memory still lives in jazz, however. His emphasis on the blues, his style of instrumentation, his freewheeling improvisations helped set New Orleans jazz on its historic course. He is remembered, too, in the titles of jazz compositions—among them, the "Buddy Bolden Stomp" and "I Thought I Heard Buddy Bolden Say."

The man who inherited Bolden's title was Freddie Keppard, another cornet player of great prowess. Keppard was a Creole Negro of mixed African and French ancestry. Such Negroes had long enjoyed exceptional privileges in New Orleans. They had lived as free men in slave days and had become skilled tailors, carpenters and musicians. After the Civil War, the fortunes of this group declined, but there were still many colored Creole families who could afford to send their sons to music teachers for formal instruction. These academically trained boys sometimes scorned the blues and ragtime of uptown Negroes, but more often they were attracted to them and learned to swing along with musicians who couldn't read a note. They brought technique and discipline to New Orleans jazz.

Keppard led the Olympia Band, which included some well-trained musicians. Keppard himself was no reader, but he had a beautiful clear tone—from all accounts—and a remarkable range. He could play tones so low he sounded like a trombone or soar above high E. If Freddie came up against a tune he didn't know, he suddenly developed valve trouble and had to take his horn apart while the other musicians ran through the number. He always knew his part by the second chorus.

Keppard left New Orleans about 1913 and traveled with the Original Creole Band to Chicago and New York. He is supposed to have made one of the fateful decisions of jazz history when he was with this band. In 1917 the Victor Phonograph Company invited the group to record, but Freddie was against it. "Nothin' doin', boys," he is reported to have said, "We won't put our stuff on records for everybody to steal." A few months later Victor recorded the Original Dixieland Jazz (or Jass) Band, a group of white New Orleans musicians, who won everlasting fame as the first band to make an out-and-out jazz disk. Freddie himself made only one record in his lifetime, long after he had reached his peak.

Among the notable musicians who worked with Keppard were clarinetists Alphonse Picou and Louis (Big Eye) Nelson. Like Keppard, Picou and Nelson were Creole Negroes. They carried a pure soaring tone and flashy technique into uptown jazz.

Picou was famous for his solo part in "High Society." Like most other jazz musicians, then and now, he moved around from band to band and city to city. Nelson stayed in New Orleans and made few recordings, but he is supposed to have inspired many younger clarinetists, including Sidney Bechet. Both Picou and Nelson lived to become grand old men of New Orleans jazz. When Picou died in 1961, 10,000 people jammed the streets to watch his funeral parade, led by the Eureka Brass Band and the Young Tuxedo Dixieland Band.

Another important Creole Negro musician was Emanuel Perez, a cornetist who was an excellent reader and teacher. Perez' life ran counter to the myth that all early jazzmen were rounders and drifters. He was a sober hard-working man, who saved his money and had an exemplary home life. Perez led the Imperial and Onward bands, both famed in the annals of New Orleans marching bands. He had a great reputation among other musicians but probably because of his quiet temperament was never called "King." That title passed from Freddie Keppard to Joe Oliver.

Joe Oliver, like Perez, was a man of excellent character—

kind, honest and upright. His personality was more colorful, however; and he managed to be in the right spot, at the right time, with the right musicians in his band. He is famed in jazz history as the leader of the first Negro band to make a jazz recording, as one of the most influential figures in spreading New Orleans jazz northward and as the guiding spirit behind Louis Armstrong—as well as for his undisputed talent as a horn blower.

Oliver was born on a Louisiana plantation in 1885 and was brought to New Orleans as a boy. His country background had a lasting effect on his music, for Oliver composed many jazz pieces around the work songs, spirituals and rough blues he heard in early childhood.

Some accounts say that young Joe worked first in a "spasm" band. Such bands were common in the South before 1900. The players made their own instruments. They plunked on cigar-box banjos, stroked washboards with thimbles, blew into jugs and hummed through combs wrapped with thin paper. They usually managed to keep their shoulders and feet in motion at the same time—to accent the strong stomping beat. Many a future jazzman began his training in these street-corner groups.

Joe also had some conventional music lessons and learned to read notes. As a youth, he doubled between playing cornet in various bands in the Negro quarter and working as a butler for a white family. He played with such famous outfits as the Olympia, Onward, and Eagle bands, as well as with a group he organized himself.

He was a tall powerful man, and his playing reflected his great physical strength. Some of his admirers thought that his tone had as much volume as Buddy Bolden's, but that he kept it under better control. He held high notes an incredibly long time, a feat that is supposed to have thrown his audiences into a wild joy. He was also famous for "freak" effects he got from his cornet by using a variety of mutes. He could imitate a rooster crowing or a baby crying.

Oliver's period of greatest achievement came after he left New Orleans in 1918 and became the King of Chicago jazz. Long before that date, he had begun to exert a strong influence over a younger trumpet player named Louis Armstrong.

Armstrong was fifteen years younger than Oliver, whom he called "Papa Joe." Oliver befriended the younger man, gave him lessons, and got him jobs. Louis never forgot his indebtedness to his hero, although he far surpassed him as a musician in later years.

Louis Armstrong belongs in the front rank of jazz immortals. He is one of a handful of authentic geniuses who raised an earthbound music to a free-soaring art. No amount of hamming and clowning can obscure Louis' real talents. His personality has often loomed larger than his music, but his best performances have a purity, simplicity and majestic beauty that need no theatrical trappings. Louis' enormous success as a roving ambassador of good will is well known. His stature as a creative force in jazz is sometimes overlooked.

Armstrong was born in New Orleans on the Fourth of July, 1900. He was born in the heart of the Negro slums, in a section so tough it was called "the battlefield." His mother was an illiterate small-town girl who married a New Orleans turpentine worker. The family lived in a ramshackle frame house without gas or running water. In the yard there was a Chinaball tree, from which his grandmother cut switches when Louis needed a whipping.

Louis was not exactly a bad boy. He was, rather, exuberant and impulsive. His big mouth and wide grin earned him the nickname of Satchelmouth, shortened later to Satchmo. He made his way through the violent life of his neighborhood with few battle scars. From earliest childhood, he was drawn irresistibly to the music that poured from the streets and dives of the city.

Young Louis was also a regular follower of marching bands. He went to school up to the fifth grade, and his worst moments came when school interfered with his joining the "second line." Louis' hero in those days was Bunk Johnson, who played cornet with the Eagle Band.

Louis also had a thorough grounding in Negro church music. His grandmother saw to it that he went to church and Sunday school, and he sang hymns and spirituals. He and his pals also sang popular songs of the day for pennies on the streets. He danced and sang, and whistled through his fingers to imitate a clarinet. Louis sang with his eyes closed and his mouth wide open. He sang tenor—believe it or not. He didn't develop his deep gravelly growl until much later.

Poverty and hard work were taken for granted by the inhabitants of Armstrong's boyhood world. His mother had a job as a maid, and his father worked twelve hours a day at the turpentine factory; but the family barely scraped along. His father and mother were often separated, and Louis was shunted back and forth among relatives. By the time he was seven, he was selling newspapers. At nine, he worked on a coal wagon, singing out "Stove coal, lady, five cents a water bucket." His job was to fill the buckets with coal between stops.

Louis had no musical instrument and no hope of getting one until a New Year's Eve escapade landed him in the Colored Waifs' Home when he was thirteen years old. Louis celebrated New Year's Eve with a bang by shooting off a gun he found in his mother's trunk. He was arrested and hauled off to juvenile court, where the judge sentenced him to the Waifs' Home, which was a combination orphanage and reform school.

Louis loved the Home. Discipline was strict, but the boys

were taught useful trades and encouraged along musical lines if they had any talent. There was a Waifs' band that was sent all over the city to play at picnics and parades. Peter Davis, who was one of the wardens of the institution and an excellent music teacher, instructed the band. Davis gave Louis a tambourine, then a bugle and finally a cornet to play. Louis learned to read a little, practiced hard and soon developed a clean clear tone and a technical facility that convinced Mr. Davis that he had a child prodigy on his hands.

The members of the Waifs' band were not permitted to play ragtime. Louis' specialty was "Home, Sweet Home." The group also played "At the Animal's Ball" and Sousa marches. Louis cried when he was released from the Home after a year and a half. He had to leave his battered cornet behind. It's still exhibited by the institution with pride.

When Louis was fifteen he got his first professional job playing in a trio at a saloon. His boss bought him a second-hand cornet from a pawnshop. The cornet was favored in New Orleans at that time. Louis later switched to the trumpet, a close relative of the cornet.

Louis was out of practice. He hit many wrong notes, and to make matters worse, his lips became very sore. But he went to work with bulldog tenacity to improve his playing and harden his lips through long hours of practice.

He made little money at first in the saloon, and he worked days driving a coal wagon. Between hauling coal in the daytime and blowing a horn at night, he managed to support himself and help his family. Fortunately he had then—as now —an iron constitution, and he thrived on overwork.

Louis had plenty of opportunity to hear other musicians. He heard the cutting contests between rival bands on advertising wagons. He joined fellow players at their after-hours hangouts. He listened to blues pianists who drifted in from the levee camps around New Orleans. But the greatest influence on Louis at this formative period in his life was Joe Oliver. Louis tried to copy "Papa Joe's" playing style, even his dress and mannerisms. Oliver, for his part, appreciated Louis' outsize talent and helped and encouraged him.

When Oliver left for Chicago in 1918, Louis was chosen to replace him in Kid Ory's band—one of the top cornet spots in the city. Louis put a bath towel around his neck—as Joe Oliver did—and blew better than ever before. But times were bad and becoming worse for New Orleans musicians. Storyville had been shut down. Wartime restrictions had closed many theaters and dance halls. There was a lull in the all-day all-night round of gaiety that had kept the city spinning to the rhythms of early jazz. After the war, many of the city's Negro workers migrated to the North. Musicians who stayed behind, like Armstrong, had to scrabble for work.

Louis was glad when he got a chance to leave New Orleans for a while. He took a job on a big excursion boat that traveled up and down the Mississippi. In those days, a fleet of sidewheel steamers carried passengers from port to port and also provided entertainment at the stops. During the winter, these boats ran moonlight excursions from southern ports; but during the summer, they traveled far up-river.

The man in charge of the music on the boats was Fate Marable, a Negro pianist from Kentucky who had an unerring instinct for finding and recruiting the best musicians around.

Marable's outfit was a hot, blues-playing, improvising dance orchestra; but unlike Kid Ory, Marable could read music, and he insisted that the members of his band do the same. Armstrong had learned to read notes at the Waifs' Home, but the two years he spent with Marable advanced his musical education considerably. These years also took Louis out of New Orleans, for the first time in his life, to places like Memphis, St. Louis, and Davenport, Iowa, where he mixed with local musicians and learned how jazz was shaping up in the hinterland. Louis was a featured player on the boats but not a soloist. Marable's band held to the New Orleans tradition of ensemble playing. Extended solos were practically unknown in jazz until Armstrong himself changed the style a few years later in Chicago.

Armstrong played on the river boats until 1921, sandwiching in work in New Orleans cabarets between trips. He also played with Oscar (Papa) Celestin's Tuxedo Brass Band, which was considered the best marching band in New Orleans. By this time, Louis' lips were steel hard and his lungs powerful. He could hit and hold higher notes than any other cornetist around, and he used an exquisitely controlled vibrato. But more important, he had begun to compose and to invent soaring improvised passages—at once intense and lyrical—that became his trademark.

Louis' reputation traveled, and he was already a legend in Chicago when he joined Joe Oliver there in the summer of 1922. The close of the New Orleans chapter in jazz was simply the opening of an extraordinary new chapter for Louis Armstrong, in which he became the first jazz soloist to win world-wide fame.

Like all the great jazz figures, Armstrong's activities and influence extend over successive periods of jazz history. We will pick up his story again as we move into those periods.

Meanwhile, to backtrack a little, there were some talented and inventive pianists who played in New Orleans in the early days. These pianists didn't work in the bands, but flourished as soloists. They included Ferdinand (Jelly Roll) Morton, Tony Jackson, and Clarence Williams—all of whom played in Storyville cabarets until the district was closed. These men were accomplished musician-composers. New Orleans also supported a floating population of rough-and-ready blues pianists who played in the cheaper dives.

Morton is the most famous of the Storyville-based pianists, largely because his life has been documented in more detail than any other musician in jazz history. He talked and played at great length for the Archives of the Library of Congress in 1938 and inspired a book, *Mister Jelly Roll*, by Alan Lomax. Jelly Roll was a Creole Negro and he liked to dwell on his French ancestry, but he was brought up by his aunt, Eulalie Echo, whom he described quite casually as a "voodoo witch."

There are wide differences of opinion about Morton's talent. From his records it seems that he was a competent ragtimer and that he was capable of giving his numbers a blues inflection—although he was scornful of what he considered crude blues. He also added imaginative Spanish tempo touches to some of his pieces, anticipating by many years such mergers in modern jazz. Jelly Roll was the composer of such classics of traditional jazz as "King Porter Stomp," "Milneburg Joys" (named after a picnic resort outside New Orleans), "Wolverine Blues," "Wild Man Blues" and "Kansas City Stomps."

Tony Jackson, who died in 1921, never made any records, but he is remembered by old New Orleans jazzmen as a great ragtime pianist. His best-known composition is "Pretty Baby."

Clarence Williams has been mentioned in the chapter on the blues. He graduated from Storyville saloons to an important career as a composer, arranger and music publisher. He accompanied Bessie Smith and directed many great jazz recording sessions in the twenties. Now more or less retired from music, Williams runs a hobby shop in Harlem.

All the musicians discussed so far happen to be Negro; but the white musicians of New Orleans were not exactly keeping their ears plugged while jazz was taking shape in their city. It was white musicians who introduced New Orleans jazz to the general public and set the style that was to be called Dixieland.

The best-known white band in New Orleans was headed by George Laine, otherwise known as Jack or "Papa." Laine's Ragtime Band was tremendously popular and in constant demand for picnics, parties and parades. Laine played military marches and rags, but he also played some of the infectious rhythms that sifted downtown from the Negro neighborhood. The band passed for all-white, but Laine actually employed two light-skinned Creole Negroes—Achille Baquet on clarinet and Dave Perkins on trombone.

Laine was born in New Orleans in 1873 and studied various instruments before he settled on drums. He organized a band before he was out of his teens and by the early 1900's had several groups working for him—both brass and dance bands.

Laine's music was undoubtedly influenced by Negro stomps and blues, just as Negro bands were influenced by military marches, quadrilles and polkas played by white musicians; but his specialty was ragtime played with a lively jerky kind of syncopation. He liked to play Scott Joplin rags, also a tune called "Praline" after a bumpy New Orleans candy made with brown sugar and pecans. "Praline" was originally a quadrille, but it kept changing as it passed back and forth between white and Negro players until it became the tune made world-famous as "Tiger Rag."

Laine broke with the European tradition of playing strictly within the confines of written notes. His dance bands played both written and "ear" music, taking their cue from improvising Negro players. All new ideas were worked out in rehearsal and then played note for note on the job. The result, nevertheless, was that Papa's boys played a much freer, fresher kind of ragtime than their competitors, and they got the best jobs.

Besides running dance bands, Papa led the famous Reliance Brass Band and also toured with his own minstrel and circus bands. His groups played on advertising wagons, at the race track and at prize fights. Almost all early white New Orleans musicians played with Laine at one time or another. Laine graduates were in the front lines of the Dixielanders who took Chicago and New York by storm at the end of World War II.

One of the stars of a Laine offshoot, the New Orleans Rhythm Kings, was Leon Rappolo. Rappolo was a fabulously talented clarinetist who influenced jazz musicians of the next two decades. His story is interesting because it shows the blending of European concert tradition and Negro folk forms that went on in New Orleans. He came from a large musical Sicilian family that had settled in and around New Orleans. His grandfather played concert clarinet. His father was a "legitimate" band leader and teacher. Leon longed to play the clarinet, not as his father did, but as he heard Negro musicians play the instrument in marching bands. His father saw to it that young Leon learned how to finger the clarinet in correct classical style, however, and made him take lessons from a man who shunned ragtime.

Leon managed nevertheless to hear the "new music" that was brewing uptown. He made friends with Creole Negro boys who knew the ragtime technique. He also managed to sneak into Storyville to hear bands like Joe Oliver's. By the time he joined the New Orleans Rhythm Kings, his playing was closer to that of Creole Negro clarinetists like Sidney Bechet and Jimmie Noone than to that of white concert musicians.

The New Orleans chapter of the jazz story ends with the exodus of its great jazz musicians. It is important to remember that the jazz that flourished in that city—vital and creative as it was—was only one stage in the long evolution of the art of jazz. We can appreciate the value of New Orleans music without stopping forever at that stage. Some people think of

New Orleans jazz, and its offspring Dixieland, as the only true jazz. They miss the excitement and beauty of the later developments. To stop at this early stage is equivalent to stopping at the works of Mark Twain in the study of American literature and never going on to Hemingway and Faulkner.

CHAPTER EIGHT

THE JAZZ EXPLOSION

The Sound of the Roaring Twenties

Until the end of the first World War, jazz was a nameless music that simmered in the American melting pot. It didn't come to a full rolling boil until the 1920's and the arrival of what writer F. Scott Fitzgerald called the Jazz Age. By then, the brew was steaming and ready for a fine noisy explosion.

There were many reasons why jazz burst on the American scene with such force at that time. First of all, there were great population shifts after the war. Thousands of Negroes left the South to find jobs in the expanding industries of northern cities, and they took with them blues and stomps and catchy dance tunes. They created an audience for jazz, often where none had existed before. Their music had an earthy vigor that ragtime lacked. At any rate, the ragtime craze was sputtering out; and white people were ready and eager to take up the infectious rhythms that filtered through to them from Negro dance halls and vaudeville houses.

Another important reason for the boom in jazz was that channels through which it could spread opened swiftly during this period. The phonograph was by then a fixture of American parlors, but until 1917 no jazz found its way onto records. The catalogues of record companies featured operatic selections by such stars as Caruso and Galli-Curci. It was a daring break from tradition when Victor issued the first jazz records, which were made by the Original Dixieland Jazz Band, a white group from New Orleans. These records sold in the millions and made jazz a household word almost overnight. The market for jazz records boomed, and all the jazz, near-jazz and would-be jazz artists of the period jumped on the bandwagon.

Radio broadcasting got under way in 1920, opening undreamed-of possibilities for the spread of the new music. In 1927, sound movies arrived. Altogether, it was a momentous decade for mass communication in America—and for jazz.

Jazz, good and bad, suited the temper of the times. The country was on a postwar binge, a binge that was to take on a hectic boom-before-the-bust quality by the late twenties. There was a feverish search for entertainment and new experiences. It was also the era of Prohibition and of big-time mobsters who made fortunes in bootleg liquor. Gangsters patronized and controlled many night clubs and speakeasies where jazzmen worked. It was a period of full but nerve-wracking employment for jazz musicians.

Prohibition also gave rise to a custom that became a necessity during Depression—the rent party. Such parties were held in private apartments to raise rent money. Any guest who could pay twenty-five cents admission was welcome. The usual feature of a rent party was a pianist who played for dancing. From the South Side of Chicago to Harlem, rent parties gave jazz pianists a chance to experiment, practice and perfect their ruggedly individual styles.

The first jazz bands to gain national fame came from New Orleans. Nick La Rocca, a graduate of Papa Laine's Reliance Band, brought a group of white New Orleans musicians to

Reisenweber's Restaurant in New York in 1917. Billed as the Original Dixieland Jazz Band, they made a sensation in New York. Jazz was certainly not unknown in New York at that time, especially among Harlem pianists; but the peppy slam-bang instrumental style of the Dixielanders was so new to Reisenweber's customers that they had to be told they could dance to it. According to one account, the patrons "after sniffing at it suspiciously like a cat with a saucer of strange food, suddenly decided that it was good and lapped it up." That same year, the group made the first of its pioneering series of jazz records.

The members of the Original Dixieland Jazz Band didn't "swing" in the modern sense. Their music leaned heavily toward ragtime. They threw in many jungle and barnyard sound effects, for jazz at that time—and for some years to come—was considered a primitive and somewhat comical affair. But to do the group justice, they were adept at the New Orleans style of improvisation—the three-way conversation of cornet, trombone and clarinet—and they were "hotter" than any other white band around. Jimmy Durante, who was beginning his career as a pianist-entertainer at that time, recalls, "It wasn't only an innovation; it was a revolution!"

The New Orleans Rhythm Kings were the second important white jazz group to go North. The Rhythm Kings (also called NORK) included three New Orleans musicians—clarinetist Leon Rappolo, trombonist George Brunis and trumpeter Paul Mares. The band played in traditional New Orleans style, and they did their best to copy the colored music they had heard at home. Their music was practically indistinguishable from that of the early Joe Oliver band. They proved that jazz could be played by talented musicians who had been sufficiently exposed to its rhythms, no matter what their skin color. The group opened at the Friars' Inn in Chicago in 1921 and were an instantaneous hit. A good recorded example of the music of the New Orleans Rhythm Kings is "Tiger Rag" (Jazz, Vol. 3, Folkways FJ 2803).

Many Negro musicians from New Orleans were already on the Chicago scene when the Rhythm Kings arrived. Chicago was the center of jazz activity in this country from 1917 to 1927. For one thing, Chicago had become the biggest railroad center in the world. Its industries drew Negro workers from all over the South, and they settled in a teeming neighborhood called the South Side. Negro blues singers and jazz musicians found there a ready-made audience, nurtured on the folk music of the rural South but eager to learn city ways. More than forty well-known New Orleans musicians moved to Chicago, some of them immediately after Storyville closed. Joe Oliver was among the first.

Louis Armstrong arrived in 1922, when Oliver sent for him to play second cornet in his band. Louis soon felt at home in Chicago. He located Brownlee's Barber Shop, a landmark for musicians from the South, and found the place filled with "home boys." Mrs. Oliver cooked him New Orleans style red beans and rice. What's more, Lil Hardin, who was the pianist with Oliver's band, took a special interest in him and was soon trying to advance his career. Lil was a classically trained musician who had left Fisk University to become a jazz pianist. She practiced with Louis to perfect his sight reading. She also interested him in the "legitimate" technique of horn blowing, and he took a few lessons from a German teacher.

Louis didn't play solos during this period. The Oliver band still used New Orleans ensemble style. Nevertheless, Louis' pure soaring tone, his warmth and exuberance soon made him the idol of the Chicago jazz world. He and Oliver played cornet duets in the breaks that were wonderfully inventive and exciting. The band began to record in 1923. Some critics consider these records the best made in the New Orleans traditional style. Examples can be found in both the Riverside History of Classic Jazz and the Folkways Jazz series.

Lil and Louis were married early in 1924. Lil felt that Louis didn't have full scope for his talent playing second cornet in Oliver's band. She engineered his going to another South Side dance hall as first cornet, and he began to shine as a soloist. He could at last let loose with the joyful improvisations that became his trademark. He became so well known that he received an invitation to join Fletcher Henderson's band in New York.

Henderson was a pace-setter in jazz in many ways. He led the first Negro jazz band to specialize in written arrangements; he was a pioneer in the big-band field; and he was the prophet of "swing." The Henderson band, when Louis joined it, was playing for white dancers at the Roseland Ballroom on Broadway.

Armstrong didn't feel completely at ease in his new surroundings. Henderson at that time favored complicated orchestrations. Louis could read the notes all right, but he felt that he couldn't "stretch out." The year he spent in New York was far from wasted, however. He put new fire into the Henderson band, and he made a number of important recordings with vocalists and small groups.

Louis backed blues singers Ma Rainey, Bessie Smith and Chippie Hill during this period. He also recorded with a small group called the Red Onion Jazz Babies, which included his wife, Lil, and several famous New Orleans jazzmen. These small group records mark an important transition from the ensemble style of New Orleans to greater emphasis on the solo in jazz performance. They also brought Armstrong to the attention of European jazz fans.

At the end of the year, Lil, once more managing his career, arranged to have Louis come back to Chicago and appear at the Dreamland Café as the "World's Greatest Jazz Cornetist."

Louis doubled between the café and the pit orchestra at the Vendome movie house.

Louis switched from the cornet to the trumpet while he was at the Vendome, not because of the sound but because he thought the trumpet, which is bigger, looked more impressive on the stage. He also introduced "scat" choruses during vocals —a wild jumble of nonsense syllables that gave him freedom to use his voice like a horn. With scat singing, a line of jazz development came full cycle. The earliest horn players in jazz imitated the human voice; they phrased their music and even breathed as vocalists did. Louis Armstrong slipped easily from vocal-style horn to horn-style vocal.

At the same time, Louis was cutting the famous Hot Five and Hot Seven records that established him once and for all as one of the great creative talents of jazz. The men who joined him on these disks included Kid Ory on trombone, Baby Dodds on drums, Johnny Dodds on clarinet and Earl Hines on piano. The sessions were so relaxed and informal that the group ruined several sides by "bustin' out laughing." These recordings are now included in a set of four long-playing disks, "The Louis Armstrong Story" (Columbia CL 851-854).

Meanwhile, Louis switched to still another South Side dance hall, the Sunset, where his name went up in lights for the first time. He played at the Vendome movie house in the afternoon and early evening, and then rushed over to the Sunset and played until dawn. Fortunately, Louis still had the iron constitution that had enabled him to dash from job to job when he was a boy in New Orleans. There were often jam sessions at the Sunset after other dance halls and cabarets closed. One legendary jazzman who jammed with Louis whenever he was in town was Bix Beiderbecke.

It is hard to separate fact from fiction when writing about Bix. He was a young cornetist from Davenport, Iowa, who lived out his short life among the great jazz talents of his day but surpassed them all in his drive for perfection. He is remembered as a legendary tragic hero of the Jazz Age.

Leon Bismarck Beiderbecke was born in Davenport in 1903. The third of three children of a prosperous German-American couple, Bix lived in a comfortable big frame house in a quiet neighborhood. He showed a precocious interest in the piano as soon as could reach the keyboard. By the age of three, he could pick out melodies with one finger. When he was seven, he played so many selections—entirely by ear—that the local paper called him a musical wonder.

Bix's parents were cultivated people, and they were pleased with this show of musical talent. They arranged music lessons for him; but Bix was resistant to learning notes or playing by any rules other than his own, and the teacher soon gave up. Left to his own devices, Bix continued to doodle at the piano. He took up the cornet in 1918, when his big brother came home from the army and bought a phonograph and a stack of records. Bix got hold of a secondhand cornet and taught himself to play along with the records. His model was Nick La Rocca of the Original Dixieland Jazz Band, and his favorite tune was "Tiger Rag."

Davenport was then a bustling river town, the end of the route for many musicians from New Orleans, Memphis and St. Louis who worked their way up the Mississippi. Showboats and excursion steamers with dance bands aboard tied up at the city's docks. One New Orleans cornetist who played in Davenport and made a tremendous impression on Bix was Emmet Hardy, a man who never recorded and is practically unknown today.

During these years, Bix was entirely self-taught and picked up a "wrong" method of fingering the cornet that was to stay with him for the rest of his life. It's impossible to say whether

Bix would have been helped or hindered if he had learned to play the cornet in the conventional way.

Bix started high school in Davenport, but he was so pre-occupied with music that he paid little attention to his studies. His family decided to send him to Lake Forest Academy just north of Chicago. They hoped to remove him from jazz influences, but Bix spent most of his time in Chicago listening to the New Orleans Rhythm Kings and South Side Negro bands. He soon convinced the faculty at the school that it was useless to keep him on the rolls. He stayed in the city and began jobbing around with a group of young musicians who called themselves the Wolverines.

The Wolverines are considered by some jazz writers the third great white band of jazz. Their music may sound choppy to modern ears, but they had plenty of enthusiasm. More important, they had Bix—whose style had already achieved a driving clarity and intensity. His cornet passages stood out in cool relief against the superheated arrangements of the band.

While Bix was with the Wolverines he traveled the college prom circuit. At one dance at Indiana University, according to a spectator, "the entire campus tried to jam into one fraternity house to hear the music." Hoagy Carmichael, a student at the university, arranged the date and became Bix's friend.

What was Bix like as a person? The men who knew him best at this time in his life remember him as deeply reserved, completely wrapped up in music, and yet kind and generous to a fault. He could never say "no" to convivial friends, and consequently seldom got the privacy he needed to practice and compose. Physically, he was short and stocky, with a round country-boy face. He had an air of needing looking-after that was very appealing to girls.

Bix was absent-minded to the point of oddity. He could never keep a coat or hat. He once packed his trunk and shipped it to another town forgetting to leave anything for himself to wear. He was absent-minded, too, about his own physical welfare. He seemed completely indifferent to ordinary routines of eating and sleeping. But Bix was a good athlete—he played golf and baseball—and had a basically rugged constitution that could take a lot of punishment. It is true that he drank a quantity of Prohibition gin, but so did many of his contemporaries who lived to ripe old ages.

Bix toured with the Wolverines until 1925, then went to St. Louis with a band organized by Frank Trumbauer, a brilliant saxophonist. He made his best recordings with Trumbauer. The stay in St. Louis also gave him a chance to go to symphony concerts; and he heard the works of Ravel, Debussy and Stravinsky—all of whom deeply affected his musical development. According to a friend in Trumbauer's band, Bix wore out a record of Stravinsky's "Firebird Suite" in St. Louis. He was inspired by Debussy's harmonic ideas and worked intuitively toward tonal effects that are only now being fully explored in jazz.

From Trumbauer's band, Bix joined Jean Goldkette's band, then Paul Whiteman's. As he changed jobs, the bands became bigger and more commercial. In records made with these groups, Bix's clean lyrical cornet passages wing out of the surrounding smog with dazzling impact.

In spite of his beautiful performances, Bix had many anxieties. The Whiteman band had a regular radio program as well as a strenuous dance schedule, which meant that the musicians constantly rehearsed new numbers. Always a slow reader, Bix found it hard to keep up with Whiteman's overdressed arrangements. He turned more and more to the piano —always his refuge in times of stress.

In 1927, Bix recorded his own piano composition, "In a Mist," which reminds us of the music of the American classical composer, MacDowell, more than it does jazz. "In a Mist" has a delicate melancholy that suggests that the composer himself was in a mist, searching for a beauty that eluded him.

The last few years of Bix's life were a downhill slide. He lost his life's savings in the financial crash of 1929 and was broke most of the time from then on. He became increasingly unreliable about filling engagements, more withdrawn, more careless than ever of his own physical welfare. In 1931, when he was twenty-eight years old, he died of pneumonia that developed from a bad cold. One of Bix's close friends stated it another way, "Die of a cold? Bix didn't die of a cold. He died of *everything*."

Bix was never well known during his lifetime except among a handful of musicians and fans. After his death, a group of young men from Princeton University, where Bix had often played, began to collect his records. A cult, in which Bix's music, his personality and his sad life story were intertwined, began to build.

Bix's legacy is a number of records which come brightly alive whenever his horn flashes out of the ensemble. The recordings generally considered his best, "Singin' the Blues" and "I'm Comin' Virginia," can be found in "The Bix Beiderbecke Story (Columbia CL 845)."

Jazz musicians of his own time, and later, were very much affected by Bix's way of playing and his striving for perfection. He especially impressed a group of young musicians who were students at Chicago's Austin High School. These boys, known as the Austin High Gang, were young teen-agers when they formed their first band in 1922.

There were five boys in the original Austin High Gang—Jimmy and Dick McPartland, Bud Freeman, Frank Teschemacher and Jim Lannigan. All the boys came from comfortable middle-class homes, and all except one had studied violin. Their approach to jazz was a mixture of adolescent revolt and genuine talent. They learned Dixieland numbers by playing the records of the New Orleans Rhythm Kings over and over. They heard the records Bix made with the Wolverines and discovered Joe Oliver's band. They spurned sheet music and tried to imitate their idols with a somewhat frantic blowing-the-roof-off approach.

This training school, rough as it was, started Jimmy McPartland on the road to a smooth trumpet style reminiscent of Beiderbecke's. Bud Freeman developed a light swirling style on the tenor sax and became an outstanding performer. Frank Teschemacher, who played the clarinet and was perhaps the most talented of the gang, was a true disciple of Bix. He was a hard-working perfectionist and pushed beyond the style of the New Orleans musicians who were his first models. He created a sound that was distinctively his own—a tone at times oddly plaintive, at others "dirty" and growling. Tesch died early in an automobile accident but left his mark on the clarinetists of his own and later generations.

The Austin High Gang played at teen-age dances all around Chicago, picking up extra talent from other schools. After graduation, they fanned out into a number of bands that can be loosely grouped as belonging to the Chicago School. Several of the boys took jobs in the pit band of a silent movie house. They were fired for playing a hot Dixieland number during a newsreel that showed Marshal Foch solemnly laying a wreath on the tomb of the unknown soldier.

Jimmy McPartland joined the Wolverines. Eventually, every member of the original Wolverine band was replaced by a musician who came up with the Austin High group.

Within a few years, young players of the Chicago School were making a sizeable splash in the jazz world. Eddie Condon was a member of this musical circle. Eddie, who was self-taught, played guitar semiprofessionally around Chicago by the time he was fifteen. He was a spark plug among the young jazzmen of that era. He helped organize record dates and was the co-founder of a band called the Chicagoans.

Gene Krupa and Dave Tough were the important drum talents in the group. Krupa was born and raised in Chicago, taught himself to play drums and began to work with bands as a teen-ager (he took lessons years later). Gene developed a relentless beat and introduced the extended drum solo into jazz. He was a superb showman and was to become one of the most important figures of the swing era—in fact the first drummer in jazz history to win world-wide renown. Tough has been rated the superior drummer by fellow musicians. Brilliant and sensitive, he was much ahead of his time. He pioneered in exploring complex rhythms that became fashionable much later, in the bop era. Dave was dogged by ill health, disappeared from the jazz scene for many years, then made several brief but impressive comebacks. He died in 1948, before he could take his rightful place among the modern jazzmen, with whose work he felt completely and happily at home.

Pianist Joe Sullivan was another shining light among these young musicians who were raised on Chicago Dixieland. They all recorded with various combos from 1927 to 1931—a period during which the Chicago style reached its peak.

The Austin High Gang and the musicians who played with them in public were white. The Chicago musicians' union at that time had a strict Jim Crow policy. White and Negro musicians got around these restrictions, however, by meeting after hours and jamming together at each other's homes and at small clubs. One of their favorite after-hours spots was the Apex Club, where New Orleans clarinetist, Jimmie Noone, had a small band.

Jimmie was in the early wave of New Orleans musicians to hit Chicago. His lacy elegant tone and warmth of style were much admired by younger jazzmen, including Bix Beiderbecke and Frank Teschemacher. Jimmie's pianist was Earl Hines, one of the trail blazers of jazz.

Earl Hines transformed the piano into a full-fledged member of the jazz band. Before his time, the piano had been used mainly as a solo instrument of ragtimers; when it was used in a band, it was relegated to a spot in the rhythm section. The piano lagged far behind the other instruments of jazz. It seemed impossible to produce on the keyboard the slurred notes that jazz horns took over from Negro spiritual singing and blues. For a long time, the jazz band pianist simply thumped away to keep the rhythm going. Hines was the first piano player of note to use hornlike phrasing. He is considered the founder of "trumpet style" piano.

Hines was born in 1905 in a suburb of Pittsburgh. His father was a trumpeter in a brass band and tried to teach his son to play this instrument. Earl had trouble learning to breathe properly, got disgusted, and switched to the piano. The trumpet lessons influenced his piano style, however. He says, "I decided to use the same ideas on piano—that was the reason for my 'trumpet style.' The ideas I wanted heard through the band could only be done like that." Earl's mother was an organist, and she encouraged him to study the piano in a serious way. He took lessons from a German teacher and practiced Czerny exercises by the hour. When he turned to jazz, he carried over the technique he had learned through this rigorous training. His first idols were two Pittsburgh pianists. One excelled in the right hand, the other the left. Earl copied them both. To this day, he's a true "two-handed" pianist.

When he was eighteen, Hines went to Chicago and worked at the Entertainers' Cabaret, where he played a miniature piano on wheels that he rolled from table to table. He attracted the attention of other Chicago musicians because he seemed to break through the limits of the keyboard. He made them realize that the piano had ten voices—one for each finger of the pianist's hands. Earl used these voices to explore new reaches of harmony and melody as well as rhythm. The effect was startling. Earl Hines seemed as "far-out" in the twenties as Thelonious Monk seemed in the mid-forties.

Hines played with all the well-known New Orleans musicians then on the South Side. He and Louis Armstrong greatly admired each other and began to play together in 1927. They undoubtedly influenced each other. Hines' style had the warmth of phrasing we associate with Armstrong; but it was also strutting, bright and brassy. His hands had a phenomenal reach, and he could run off a series of octave chords and tremolos that stunned his audiences.

Hines played with Jimmie Noone at the Apex Club and recorded with that group. He also made a number of classic records with Armstrong, including the famous "West End Blues" and "Muggles." For ten years, he led his own band at a Chicago night club, the Grand Terrace. He became famous during this period through nightly radio broadcasts, and he also picked up his nickname "Fatha." The story goes that he had lectured a radio announcer, in a fatherly way, about drinking on the job. The announcer promptly introduced him to the radio audience as "Fatha Hines."

Hines' influence reached far beyond the Chicago jazz scene of the twenties. He continued to set the pace for pianists through many years of jazz history.

Another famous graduate of the Chicago jazz scene is clarinetist Benny Goodman. Benny was born in Chicago and grew up at the same time as the jazz-crazy gang from Austin High School. He knew the Austin High boys and sometimes played with them at school dances, but he didn't give jazz the same kind of all-out dedication. Benny was more attracted to classical music at that time, and he stayed on the fringes of the group. He didn't make his great impact on the jazz world until he had left Chicago. Nevertheless, his style was formed in Chicago and shows clearly the influence of the great Creole Negro clarinetists who gathered there.

Benjamin David Goodman was born in Chicago in 1909, the eighth of twelve children of a poor Jewish family. His parents had fled from Russia to escape anti-Semitic violence and bitter poverty. Although they were poor in this country, they had hope for their children's future and for the miracles that could be accomplished through education. Like many other Jewish families of that era, they had faith in the power of music lessons, for they had seen Jewish boys escape from ghetto life to win fame and fortune through musical talent.

Benny's family attended free band concerts at a park near their home. His father pushed the boys in the family toward a neighborhood synagogue that gave free music lessons and supplied musical instruments. Benny played his first clarinet there. When the synagogue ran out of money to support the music program, the Goodman boys gravitated to Hull House, a famous Chicago settlement house where Benny continued to play clarinet in a boys' band.

Benny's first idol was Ted Lewis, a very popular singer-clarinetist whose jaunty manner was much imitated. When Benny was twelve years old, he earned his first money as an entertainer by imitating Lewis on the stage of a Chicago vaudeville house. Soon after, he started to take clarinet lessons from Franz Schoepp. Schoepp was a stern disciplinarian, who gave his students a thorough training in the "legitimate" style of clarinet playing. He had nothing but contempt for jazz. Ironically, some of the greatest clarinetists of jazz studied with him—including, besides Goodman, Buster Bailey and Jimmie Noone.

At about the same time, Benny discovered Leon Rappolo at Friars' Inn, and he was also deeply impressed by Jimmie Noone and Frank Teschemacher. Nevertheless, he wavered between jazz and classical music until he was offered a job playing three nights a week at a neighborhood dance hall. He earned forty-eight dollars a week there, a magnificent sum to a fourteen-year-old boy in knickers. When he was fifteen, he put on his first pair of long pants and traveled to the coast and back with a band organized by Ben Pollack, a drummer formerly with the New Orleans Rhythm Kings.

Benny played with various outfits around Chicago until 1929, when he went to New York and launched the musical activities that would bring him world-wide fame. His clean, bright, happy clarinet sound and his superb musicianship were soon to make him one of the greatest celebrities in jazz history. Many middle-aged people around today feel that jazz began and ended with the "King of Swing." We'll meet Benny again, as the jazz scene shifts to a new time, a new place.

CHAPTER NINE

EVERYBODY SWINGS

Big Bands and Big Names

We have seen how jazz traveled from New Orleans to Chicago, with a few side excursions, after the first World War. By the middle of the 1920's, jazz music and musicians were once again on the move. This time the magnet was New York, the new entertainment capital of the nation. Jazz musicians flocked to the city for boom-time jobs in night clubs, theaters and dance halls. The big music publishers, the major record companies and radio broadcasting studios were in New York.

The postwar wave of Negro migration from the South hit New York a little later than it did Chicago; but by the time Negro jazz musicians began to congregate in Harlem, the neighborhood was bursting at its seams and rocking with a steady beat. Great ragtime and stride pianists roamed the rent party circuit, which became an informal training school for young musicians.

Racial barriers in jazz were beginning to break down; and when "swing" arrived, it was a product of Negro and white musicians, influencing each other and, by the mid-thirties, working together. Swing was the main stream of jazz from

1935 until World War II. It swept jazzmen to unprecedented material success and made a segment of jazz *the* popular music of the American people. Benny Goodman was the "King of Swing," but his kingdom didn't appear overnight. It had been building gradually for at least a decade.

The man who set the stage for the swing era was Fletcher Henderson, leader of the first jazz band that can be described as both *big* and *hot*. Fletcher was an unlikely candidate for jazz fame when he arrived in New York in 1920. He was a tall, scholarly-looking, mild-mannered young man, who came up from Georgia to do graduate work in chemistry. His father was a school principal, his mother a pianist and music teacher. His mother had taught him to play piano, but no one thought that Fletcher would make a career of it.

To help pay his school expenses, Fletcher took a part-time job as a song demonstrator for a New York music publishing house. He was soon promoted to the full-time post of house pianist at a recording studio owned by the same company. That was the end of his chemistry studies.

One of the recording artists he worked with was Ethel Waters, then a leading blues singer. He organized a small band to tour with her to promote her records. Miss Waters later claimed that she shook Fletcher loose from a somewhat academic piano style during this tour by making him listen to the piano rolls of James P. Johnson.

Henderson was not a great pianist. He played piano accompaniments for dozens of blues singers, and he played the piano with his band; but he never featured himself as a soloist. When he had to record a number with a good part for a solo pianist, he was apt to call in his friend Fats Waller.

Fletcher's great achievement was working out the pattern of big-band jazz. He had a wonderful ear for jazz talent. He was a gifted arranger, too, as his arrangements for Benny Goodman in the thirties were to prove. During the early history of the Henderson band, Don Redman, a brilliant conservatory-trained saxophonist, did the arranging; but Henderson's taste and ideas were evident.

Fletcher's first important break came in 1924 when he was hired to lead a band at Roseland, a huge dance palace on Broadway. He brought a nine-piece band into Roseland and introduced a new style of jazz orchestration. Before his time there had been efforts to write arranged jazz for large groups, but the results were very unjazzlike. Fletcher treated the sections of his big band as though they were individual instruments of a small group. He used brass and reed sections as separate voices, pitting them against each other in call-and-response form. He left room for improvisation, too, in solo passages against an arranged background. This was quite a departure from the one-of-a-kind instrumentation and group improvisation of New Orleans days—a style that had dominated jazz until Fletcher's time.

Louis Armstrong joined the Henderson band during Fletcher's first year at Roseland, and it's generally agreed that the band really took fire during his stay. Through Armstrong, the best of the New Orleans tradition fused with swing at its very beginning. Don Redman found that he had to make the band arrangements hotter and more rhythmic to suit Louis' style. Louis left Henderson to return to Chicago at the end of a year, but he left an indelible stamp on the band.

Henderson played at Roseland on and off for the next fifteen years. Armstrong was only one of the many illustrious jazzmen to play with the band. Coleman Hawkins, the man who made a real jazz instrument out of the tenor sax, played with Henderson for a decade.

The sax was a slow starter in jazz. Although the instrument had been around since the 1840's and was widely used in brass bands, it was thought unsuitable for jazz until the mid-twenties. Hawkins was the only important tenor saxophonist playing jazz when he joined Fletcher in a recording date in 1923. He played with a big warm tone that set the standard for the instrument for years afterward. Hawkins had advanced melodic and harmonic ideas that were to keep him in the forefront of jazz through many changes of style. His biggest single hit—recorded in 1939—was a beautiful treatment of "Body and Soul."

The Roseland Ballroom kept two bands going, one Negro and one white. Some of the most important white jazzmen of the era shared the twin bandstands with Henderson. There were many cutting contests between the two groups. Before a musical battle, Fletcher would say to his men, "Come on— let's take charge," and they would try to blow the house down.

After the ballroom closed at 1:00 o'clock, Fletcher often went up to Harlem to play at dances there until the early hours of the morning. In the late twenties, the Savoy Ballroom was the home of the Lindy Hop, a dance with a strong off-beat rhythm which seemed made for Fletcher's music (and vice-versa.) Fletcher also played at the Apollo vaudeville house on 125th Street, a great showcase in those days for Negro bands.

Musicians felt that it was an honor to play with Henderson. Those who measured up to his high musical standards found him a fair and generous leader. Never a self-promoter, Fletcher let the members of the band take the limelight, and he did everything possible to exploit their names. The spirit of the band in its heyday was very happy.

Henderson was not a good businessman, however. He got by in good times but couldn't hold the band together during the Depression. His musicians were devoted to him, but they had to admit defeat after several very lean years. The band simply disintegrated in the mid-thirties.

Meanwhile, the migrations of jazzmen to New York from

other parts of the country had been stepped up. Benny Goodman arrived in Manhattan in 1929 and for several years freelanced around the city. In 1934 he won national attention with his own band on a regular radio show called "Let's Dance."

Goodman knew and appreciated Fletcher Henderson's work. Fletcher arranged much of Goodman's best material during the next few years.

✳Benny Goodman came along at the right time with the right organization to make big-band jazz a national craze. The lilting sound of his clarinet ushered in the age of swing. "Jitterbugs" of the 1930's jammed the Paramount Theater in New York when Benny played there. As Benny recalls it, when the band came up on a rising platform between movies, the sound from the audience was "like Times Square on New Year's Eve." Teen-agers did the Shag and the Big Apple in the aisles, and it took a whole platoon of ushers to keep order. Through all the furor, Benny was dignified and composed— looking much more like a successful businessman than the popular image of a jazzman.

As the "King of Swing," Benny brought jazz to the largest audience in its history. He built an international reputation, which in years to come was to make him a valuable ambassador of good will for the American government. Benny also made a lasting contribution to jazz by breaking down the Jim Crow practices usual in bands before his time. He was the first well-known white band leader to hire Negro musicians. He introduced Teddy Wilson, Lionel Hampton, Charlie Christian and many other topflight Negro players to the general public. Because of his own tremendous popularity, Benny could break taboos which had long worked to the disadvantage of both races.

From a purely musical viewpoint, Benny also made jazz progress by experimenting with small instrumental groups. From 1935 on, he formed many such groups—ranging from trios to septets—within his band. Some of his best recordings were made with these units.

Fletcher Henderson played piano with Benny's band for a brief period in 1939 but then returned to leading his own band. His new group made little impression, and Fletcher worked only intermittently in music until his death in 1952. John Hammond has since put together a fine album of Henderson recordings titled "The Fletcher Henderson Story" (Columbia C4L 19).

After Benny Goodman led the way, a number of other white band leaders rode the wave of swing to fame and fortune. At the first so-called swing concert in New York in 1936, Glen Gray's Casa Loma Orchestra, and groups led by Tommy Dorsey and Artie Shaw were on the program. Gray's band (named after the Casa Loma Hotel in Toronto where the group had its start) was extremely popular in college circles in the thirties and made many hit records.

Tommy Dorsey played the trombone, and his brother Jimmy played clarinet and alto sax. The Dorseys, together and separately, led many popular dance groups from the early thirties to the mid-fifties. Born in Shenandoah, Pennsylvania, where their father was a music teacher, they were raised on music; and both were exceptional instrumentalists. The Dorseys' music was known to millions through records and radio and television programs.

It's impossible to mention all the popular bands of the swing era. Red Nichols, Glenn Miller, Bunny Berigan, Harry James and many others had ardent fans who collected their recordings and flocked to the ballrooms where they played.

One band of the swing school kept a little ahead of jazz trends as they developed in the forties. This was the Woody Herman band. Woody was born in Milwaukee in 1913, and he played clarinet and sax with various outfits for years, until he hit the big-time with his record of "Woodchopper's Ball" in 1939.

Woody has had his own radio program, made a State Department sponsored tour of Latin America, and has won many honors and awards.

The Herman bands have been notably adventurous in exploring new rhythms. Igor Stravinsky is said to have been enchanted by Woody's "Caldonia," which is full of rhythmic surprises. Stravinsky composed "Ebony Concerto" specifically for Woody in 1945.

William (Chick) Webb led one of the most memorable bands of the thirties. A powerful pulsating drummer, Chick was the uncrowned king of the Savoy Ballroom in Harlem during the years when the Lindy Hop was at its peak. Anyone who visited the Savoy during those years remembers the electric exchange between the musicians on the bandstand and the dancers on the floor as they set a fantastic pace for each other.

Chick was a gallant little man who overcame deformity and pain to become a great jazz performer. He was born badly crippled and couldn't walk at all for many years. An operation finally enabled him to use his feet and to play drums, but he remained hunchbacked and frail. His memorable career was cut short by death in 1939 when he was thirty-seven years old.

One of the things best known about Chick is that he discovered Ella Fitzgerald in an amateur contest at a Harlem theater. Ella was sixteen years old at the time, a shy awkward girl from Yonkers, New York. Chick was so impressed by her lovely voice that he hired her to work with the band. She made her first professional appearance in a dress borrowed from Chick's wife.

Ella is usually considered the best of all popular singers rather than a true jazz performer. The dividing line, in her case, is not very distinct. She infuses a wide range of ballads and show tunes with a true jazz feeling and is capable of using her voice—as in her famous scat choruses of "Lady Be Good" and "How High the Moon"—as a superb improvising horn.

The only band leader who ever successfully challenged Chick Webb at the Savoy was Count Basie. Basie led one of the greatest of all big jazz bands. Arriving later on the scene than Fletcher Henderson, Basie didn't have to blaze a new trail. He simply played in swing style better than anyone else around. The Basie band included some remarkable instrumentalists and singers, who worked together with a joyous romping spirit. The band's trademark, then and later, was a free-flowing rhythm section pushed along in masterly fashion by Basie's piano.

Basie spent his formative years as a band leader in Kansas City and gathered many of his musicians from that section of the country; but his birthplace was in the East. He was born William Basie in Red Bank, New Jersey. His mother was musically inclined and gave him his first piano lessons. He later studied with a German music teacher. (Such teachers have wielded a strong if unwitting influence on jazz. Many a jazzman learned his musical ABC's from a German-born teacher who was a strict classicist.)

Bill Basie lived near enough to New York to gravitate to Harlem when he was a teen-ager. His first idol was James P. Johnson, the dean of Harlem pianists. Johnson had enormous talent as a pianist and composer and was the founder of the "stride" school of piano—in which the left hand pounds out a powerful bass, alternating single notes and chords. He helped along many of the younger pianists who roamed the rent party circuit during the twenties.

But the pianist who most influenced Basie was another young disciple of Johnson's, Thomas (Fats) Waller. Waller was an enormously gifted pianist, the writer of an endless stream of tunes—many of which became jazz classics—and a witty, charming and wildly irrepressible entertainer. He was, besides, a basically serious musician who was most contented when he was playing Bach fugues on the organ. But Fats' clowning sometimes got in the way of his music. His son Maurice stated it this way: "He was a remarkable musician, my father. He had, however, a terrific personality that over-lorded his true greatness at the piano."

Thomas Waller was born in New York in 1904. His father was the minister of the Abyssinian Baptist Church and wanted his son to follow in his footsteps. But Fats, who was the youngest of twelve children, showed musical leanings from earliest childhood. His mother, to whom he was devoted, played piano and organ. He took up the piano and by the time he was fifteen could play well enough to work as a professional. Fats' first job was at the Lincoln Theater, where Basie met him.

Fats had a wide-ranging piano style. He could be all power and drive, or he could play with astonishing delicacy. He was a fantastically fast composer. He wrote three hit tunes, including "Honeysuckle Rose," in one two-hour session; and he tossed off "Ain't Misbehavin'" in forty-five minutes. It wasn't unusual for Fats to write a show tune during a final rehearsal or to compose a new piece for recording when he got to the studio.

Money slipped out of his hands. He was often hard up and sold many of his songs for absurdly small amounts. Fats made so many records and broadcasts, wrote so many songs and appeared in so many shows here and abroad that the pace became frantic. He was always surrounded by hordes of friends for whom he played the role of both king and jester. He relied more and more on whiskey to ease the tension as time went on.

Waller continued to love to play the organ but seldom got

a chance to play this instrument in public. He once climbed to the loft of the Cathedral of Notre Dame in Paris and took turns playing the organ with the cathedral's organist. He also played the organ at a Cincinnati radio station, without billing, in the early hours of the morning after singing and clowning on a late night program called "Fats Waller's Rhythm Club."

Fats died in 1943 shortly after he appeared in *Stormy Weather*, the most successful of several movies he made during his lifetime. He left a rich legacy of laughter and music. "Every time someone mentions Fats Waller's name," says Louis Armstrong, "why you can see the grins on all the faces . . ." James P. Johnson, who was inconsolable at Waller's death, said: "Some little people has music in them, but Fats, he was *all* music, and you know how big he was."

Bill Basie was profoundly influenced by Waller but traveled quite a different path in his career. He worked with singers and vaudeville acts, using New York as a base, for several years. Then he took a job with a touring vaudeville show that got as far as Kansas City and folded. Basie was broke and had no way to get home. He stayed in Kansas City and joined a band led by pianist Bennie Moten.

Kansas City in the thirties was a musicians' town. It attracted jazzmen from all over the South and Southwest. The Negro neighborhood swarmed with musicians who carried their horns with them, and there were fabulous jam sessions, day and night.

Basie was ready to try his hand at leading by 1935. He organized a band that included blues singer Jimmy Rushing, who was to be a mainstay of the group for fifteen years, and drummer Jo Jones. The band settled down in a cabaret known as the Reno Club and started to broadcast over a small Kansas City radio station.

Basie got the name "Count" while he was at the Reno Club. A radio announcer decided to promote him to the ranks of

jazz royalty that already included Earl Hines and Duke Ellington. He introduced Basie over the air as "Count." The
name stuck professionally, but Basie's friends have always
called him Bill.

The style that Basie established as his own during the late
thirties is the style that still identifies him today. It's a style
rooted in the blues and improvised "ear" music. What makes
the Basie sound so distinctive is the rhythm—four solid beats
to the bar laid down by a rugged rhythm section. "I don't
dig that two-beat jive the New Orleans cats play," Basie once
remarked, "because my boys and I got to have four heavy
beats to a bar and no cheating."

Basie regards himself as part of the rhythm section. He
seems to jab at the keyboard in the most casual right-handed
manner, but he actually is the source of the band's power and
drive. He sounds exactly the right notes, at the right time, to
push the band along and ease the soloists in and out of the
ensemble.

The Basie rhythm section of guitar, string bass, drums and
piano is one of the best in jazz history. Basie has also always
featured brilliant tenor saxophonists. Lester Young, whose
light, dry, moody style was to make him the idol of a whole
new generation of sax men, worked with Basie for several
years. Other great tenor players who have worked with Basie
from time to time include Coleman Hawkins and Ben Web-
ster.

The Basie band has always been notable for its contagiously
happy mood and for the team spirit of its members. Basie
himself presides with dignity and quiet charm. He's led his
big band continuously over the past two-and-a-half decades
and gained a world-wide reputation.

Jimmie Lunceford led another big band of quality during
the swing years. Lunceford was brought up in Denver, Colo-
rado, where he took music lessons from James Wilberforce

Whiteman, father of the famous Paul. He learned to play all the reed instruments and decided to make music his career. After graduating from Fisk University in 1927, he taught music at a high school in Memphis, where he organized a student band. The band later become professional and made annual cross-country tours playing at college proms, ballrooms and theaters. Lunceford was that rarity in jazz—a baton-wielding leader. He and his trumpeter-arranger, Sy Oliver, created a relaxed, smooth, two-beat music that enjoyed a great vogue from about 1934 to 1939.

The swing bands that flourished in the mid-thirties opened the way for another and quite different jazz development— boogie woogie.

Boogie woogie is a style of blues played on the piano with a rolling eight-beats-to-the-bar bass. It's a style both primitive and complex, in which drumlike rhythms and repeated short melodic phrases create an almost hypnotic effect. No one knows exactly how far back this style goes. It flourished for some years, unnoticed by the general public, wherever Negro dancers from the Deep South wanted their music strong and hot. Unlike ragtime, boogie was invented by men who knew nothing about classical music. Their numbers took the form of the twelve-bar blues, repeated with endless variations.

Boogie woogie came dramatically into the spotlight at a concert, "Spirituals to Swing," given in New York in 1938; but a man named Jimmy Yancey had been playing in this style in Chicago at least fifteen years before. Yancey was a self-taught pianist as well as a tap dancer and singer. As a child, he played in stage shows, traveled widely in this country and visited the capitals of Europe. In the late teens, Yancey settled down in Chicago's South Side and became a popular pianist at rent parties and dances.

Yancey worked against a background of blues and rags,

but he also used rhythmic effects that seem purely African. His "Yancey Stomp" has a rhythmic drive that reminds us of the stomping and clapping of an old-time ring shout.

Yancey never became as well known as two younger pianists he inspired—Albert Ammons and Meade Lux Lewis. Ammons and Lewis drove taxicabs for a Chicago company around 1924. They were both more interested in piano playing than cab driving. Their boss had to fix up a club room with a piano so that he could keep track of them.

Ammons was strictly an "ear" man, with a strong and joyous boogie style. Lewis had been taught violin but abandoned that instrument promptly when he heard Jimmy Yancey play. He taught himself to play piano and practiced with dogged determination until he achieved a remarkable technique.

The best known of all genuine boogie woogie pieces is Meade Lux Lewis' "Honky Tonk Train Blues." Lux's father was a Pullman porter, and the family lived near a railroad line. The rush of passing trains and the rhythmic clanking of wheels against track worked into Lux's piano piece. Using the blues form, he wove left- and right-hand rhythms together in such a complex way that it's easy to imagine that two pianists are playing.

Lewis recorded the "Honky Tonk Train Blues" for a small company in 1927. The record was not released until 1929, and the company folded shortly afterward. There the matter might have rested except for the sleuthing of John Hammond, that indefatigable discoverer of great jazz talent. Hammond happened on a battered copy of the record in 1936 and went looking for the creator. He found Lewis washing cars in a Chicago garage and persuaded him to record the piece again.

Meade Lux Lewis, Albert Ammons and Pete Johnson—a Kansas City boogie woogie artist—all played at the historic

Carnegie Hall 1938 concert in New York. Boogie woogie spread like wildfire. It dawned on the nation's music makers that the boogie beat could be applied to almost any tune— the same discovery that they had made about ragtime a quarter of a century before. The whole country rocked to such songs as "Beat Me Daddy Eight to the Bar." By 1941 boogie woogie had been literally played to death. It survives today only as an occasional side line of jazz pianists.

Another pianist who came more quietly to public notice in the swing period was Teddy Wilson. Teddy was the first Negro musician to join the Goodman band when Benny made his famous breakthrough in 1935. He became nationally known during his tours with the band during the next four years.

Wilson has had a many-faceted career. He has been continuously active on the jazz scene for over thirty years as a pianist, arranger, composer and band leader. He has also given courses at the Juilliard School of Music in New York and taught many private pupils.

Wilson had a thorough grounding in classical music before he went into the jazz field. He studied music both at Tuskegee Institute and Talladega College. He spent a few years early in his career in Chicago and played with such giants of the New Orleans school as Louis Armstrong and Jimmie Noone. He also came under the influence of Earl Hines in Chicago. But Teddy developed a style very much his own—a swinging, deceptively simple attack that caused just as much astonishment among musicians in the thirties as Hines' "trumpet" style had caused in the twenties.

Teddy Wilson achieved a fresh sound, not through fireworks, but by building a neat precise structure of single notes in the right hand over an even flowing beat. He opened the way for the pianists of the bop era.

Wilson accompanied vocalist Billie Holiday in a remarkable series of recordings made in the late thirties. Billie reached her peak in these records, of which a splendid collection can be found in "Billie Holiday—The Golden Years" (Columbia C3L 21). Billie rates next to Bessie Smith as a great jazz vocalist. She sang many non-jazz songs and ballads, but she could infuse the most ordinary Tin Pan Alley number with the tone color and off-beat phrasing of jazz. She used her strange harsh-sweet voice like a horn. As she stated it herself:

> I don't think I'm singing. I feel like I'm playing a horn. I try to improvise like Les Young, like Louis Armstrong, or someone else I admire. What comes out is what I feel. I hate straight singing. I have to change a tune to my own way of doing it. That's all I know.

The story of Billie's trouble-ridden life has often been told. She had a bitter impoverished childhood, relieved only by her devotion to her mother and her mother's devotion to her. She was inspired by the records of Bessie Smith which she heard as a child. She started singing in gin mills and night clubs while she was still in her teens and came to the attention of discriminating jazz fans.

Billie made records with Benny Goodman and Teddy Wilson that brought her international fame. She also toured as featured vocalist with Count Basie and Artie Shaw. She made a vivid impression on her audiences. A beautiful woman, she customarily wore a white evening dress and tucked a white gardenia into her hair.

Somewhere along the way, Billie became addicted to drugs and began an agonizing downhill course in both her personal life and career. As Billie summed it up, "All dope can do for you is kill you—and kill you the long slow hard way. And it can kill the people you love right along with you." Billie fought a losing battle against her addiction. The battle ended in 1959 in a Manhattan hospital where she died at the age of forty-five.

Another great talent, who burst on the jazz scene of the thirties like a skyrocket, was Art Tatum. Tatum was a pianist of almost unbelievable technical brilliance. He went so far beyond other pianists in sheer speed and dexterity at the keyboard that no one tried to match him.

Tatum came from Toledo, Ohio, where he made his professional bow as staff pianist at a local radio station. He later made New York his home base. He was a big, amiable, confident man—almost blind—whose whole life revolved around playing the piano. He was at his best in the back rooms of Harlem saloons where musicians gathered to hear each other after working hours. Tatum would sit down at the piano late at night and play right through the early hours of the morning. One legend tells of his playing forty-eight hours at a stretch.

Tatum loved the after-hours sessions, where he could play whatever he pleased for as long as he pleased, surrounded by his friends; but he also made many public appearances. He starred at the Onyx Club on 52nd Street in Manhattan, where a number of well-known concert musicians came to hear him. He also led small groups in Chicago and New York and made many recordings. Verve has issued a monumental series of Tatum disks under the title of "The Genius of Art Tatum."

Tatum died in California in 1956. His exact niche in jazz history is not yet clear. Some critics consider his style over-ornamented and pretentious; others point to its delicacy and subtlety. Toward the end of his life, Tatum worked on ideas of pitch and harmony far advanced for his time.

And now—finally—Duke Ellington. Duke has been left for last in this chapter on pre-swing and full-swing jazz, because he doesn't fit neatly into any of the usual pigeonholes. Ellington is one of the true titans of jazz. He has been a leading figure of the jazz world for more than thirty-five years. He has adapted to new vogues in jazz as they have come along, but there is only one word for his basic style—and that's "Ellingtonian."

Duke is a tall, handsome, courtly man who is calmly aware of his own talent. He is technically a pianist, but his real instrument is his orchestra. He has led the same group of men for so long that the whole orchestra seems fused into one remarkable voice. Duke is happiest when this voice is sounding all around him. The Ellington orchestra keeps up a pace of record making, broadcasts and one-night stands that would be killing for an ordinary group.

Edward Kennedy Ellington was born in Washington, D. C., in 1899. His father made blueprints for the Navy Department, and the family was modestly well-to-do. Young Edward was always well dressed—so well dressed, in fact, that his schoolmates nicknamed him "Duke."

Duke started to take piano lessons when he was six years old. As he grew up, he showed promise in two fields—music and art. He went to Armstrong High, a manual training high school in Washington, where he specialized in commercial art. He was so good at painting and sketching that he was offered a scholarship at a New York art institute, but by that time he had decided in favor of music. It's interesting to note that Ellington has always been a superb "colorist" in music. His compositions are mood pictures painted with masterly brush strokes of melody, harmony and rhythm.

Duke organized a small band while he was still in high school. His early models were ragtime players, especially James P. Johnson, whose piano roll of "Carolina Shout" was Duke's favorite. The blues also attracted him. The haunting vocal style of the blues and the brooding strains of old Negro work songs and spirituals were to prove important spurs to Duke's creative imagination.

After high school, Duke enlarged his band to six pieces and took a big ad in the classified section of the Washington phone book. Ellington's Washingtonians were soon much in demand at parties and dances.

Within the next few years, Duke married, and his son, Mercer, was born. He decided that the place for an up-and-coming band was in New York. It took him a few years to become established in Manhattan. The first big landmark in his career came when his band was hired by the Cotton Club in Harlem. Duke worked at the Cotton Club from 1927 to 1932, beginning at the peak of the nation's wild spending spree. The Cotton Club was an expensive night club that catered to bootleggers, gangsters and stage celebrities. The club hired the best Negro talent in the country and had its own radio hook-up.

The patrons of the Cotton Club demanded "primitive" music, and Ellington gave them plenty of jungle sound. He had outstanding plunger-mute men in the brass section, who made their horns growl and moan with blood-curdling effect. The miracle is that the band continued to play real jazz of high quality and that Duke turned out a number of original compositions and brilliant recordings during this period. By the time the stock market crashed, he had an international reputation. His band was one of the few in the business that was steadily employed through the Depression.

One of the high points of Duke's career was a 1943 concert at Carnegie Hall in New York. This was the event that some jazz historians feel turned the whole tide of jazz—changing it from dance music to concert music. Duke presented a new work, "Black, Brown and Beige," to a serious and attentive audience in evening dress. The composition told the story of the Negro people in America in moving musical terms. The piece ran for fifty minutes and was Duke's most ambitious and successful attempt to that date to break through the time restrictions set by popular songs and phonograph records. Such compositions in jazz are said to be in "extended form." They are as commonplace today as they were rare in 1943. If Ellington is indeed responsible for making the jazz audience sit down, it is ironic, for Duke likes to play for dancing to this day.

It is estimated that eighteen million Ellington records have been sold since he made his first disk in 1924. One legendary collection was made by the late King George V of England, who was said to own more Ellington records than Duke himself. New compositions and arrangements have rolled in an endless stream out of the Ellington mill. Some Ellington tunes are "Solitude," "Sophisticated Lady," "Mood Indigo," "Don't Get Around Much Anymore," "I'm Beginning to See the Light," and there are many many more. Duke himself estimates that he has written fifteen hundred songs.

In 1939, Billy Strayhorn, an extremely talented composer-arranger, joined Ellington. Duke gave Strayhorn only one order when he joined the band: "Observe." Strayhorn has written or collaborated on much of the orchestra's material through the years. He is the composer of the well-known Ellington theme, "Take the A Train." He and Duke work together so closely that they often don't know who wrote what.

Ellington does most of his composing on the move, especially in trains. Trains put him in the right creative mood. As he explains it, "When I board a train, peace descends on me, the train's metallic rhythm soothes me. The fireman plays blues on the engine whistle. . . ."

When Duke composes, he writes to individuals in his orchestra rather than to instruments. He uses the many different tone colors to be found in the band as part of the total composition. The famous Ellington sound, never successfully imitated, comes from the artful blending of these different timbres.

Great stars of Duke's band include the late Bubber Miley, an artist at producing trumpet growls with a rubber plunger mute, and "Tricky Sam" Nanton, famous for his wa-wa trombone sound. Harry Carney, master of the strong virile baritone saxophone, joined Ellington in 1926 and is still a mainstay of the band; so is Johnny Hodges, who joined the band in 1928 and is noted for his slow melodic solos on alto sax. Trumpeter "Cootie" Williams, for whom Ellington wrote "Concerto for Cootie," was in the ensemble through the thirties. Paul Gonsalves, a tenor sax man in the Coleman Hawkins tradition, has been with Ellington for over ten years. He leaped to fame when he created a riot at a Newport Jazz Festival in 1956 by playing a twenty-seven-chorus solo. It's impossible to list all the jazz greats who have been with Ellington at one time or another. Most of them have stayed for stretches of time unparalleled in the history of jazz bands.

At a number of times in the past, critics have decided that Ellington was past his peak; but each time, before they could write him off, Duke embarked on some new musical adventure. Recently he has been involved in the problems of composing under and around dialogue for movies and television. "I like to have problems," Duke says, "otherwise everything gets routine and I get lazy."

Duke says of present-day jazz, "It's grown up so much that it's pretty hard to draw the line as to what is jazz and what isn't. It's just, 'does it sound good?'—that's the basis of all music. If it sounds good it is good."

A good sampling of basic Ellington that both *is* jazz and

sounds good is "The Music of Duke Ellington" (Columbia CL 558). For advanced Ellington, listen to the orchestra play selections from Grieg's "Peer Gynt Suites" with "Suite Thursday" on the reverse side. Ellington at his most experimental is a good introduction to the world of modern jazz.

CHAPTER TEN

THE BOP REVOLUTION

Bird and Dizzy Lead the Way

We live in a remarkable age of jazz. The music is more exciting and adventurous than ever and offers great rewards to
those who listen with open ears—and open minds. There's a
new breed of jazzmen on the scene, men who have studied
the theory as well as the practice of music in colleges and
music schools across the country and who apply advanced
ideas of melody, harmony and rhythm to the old folk-based
materials of jazz. These musicians are traveling at what may
at times seem breakneck speed to overtake 700 years of
achievement in classical music. They seldom play tunes that
are easy to hum or whistle, they use chords that may sound
strange on first hearing, and they juggle rhythms in a complicated way.

We will see how these new ideas evolved, starting with the
"bop" revolution of the early forties. The bop music of Charlie
Parker and Dizzy Gillespie drew howls of rage from critics
and public alike when it first burst on the musical scene, but
within a few years it sounded "right" and beautiful.

Bop (or as it was called earlier, rebop or bebop) was a

major musical upheaval. It laid the foundation for all modern jazz. It was the product of a group of serious and remarkably talented musicians, and it took shape around 1940 in small Harlem cafés patronized mainly by jazzmen. Bop didn't reach the general public until the mid-forties, and then it was all but swamped by bad publicity. Magazines and newspapers played up the supposedly weird language and mannerisms of bop and popularized a comic-strip version of the bop musician, complete with horn-rimmed glasses, goatee and beret. Within a few years, musicians were happy to get rid of the word "bop," and the jazz that came to the fore was called "cool," "progressive" or simply "modern."

The founding fathers of bop were a group of refugees from popular swing bands. They were jazz musicians who outgrew swing. They felt hemmed in by big-band arrangements. They were frustrated by the lack of opportunity to experiment and "stretch out." These rebels began to meet after hours to jam at Harlem night spots. Minton's Play House, on West 118th Street, is famous as the cradle of bop.

The owner of the Play House, Henry Minton, had been an official of the musicians' union. He started the Play House as an informal clubhouse for his cronies, with good meals, a bar and a jukebox that blared all day long. Early in 1940, Minton persuaded a well-known former band leader, Teddy Hill, to manage the place for him, and he gave Teddy a free hand with the music policy. Teddy had a fine ear for jazz talent and a mind open to musical progress. He hired several musicians to play nights in the back room of the café and gave them an unusual amount of leeway. They could get off and on the stand when they liked, play whatever they liked and decide who could sit in with them.

The back room at Minton's quickly became a gathering place for the most advanced jazzmen of the day. Musicians beat a path there from the hotels, dance halls and radio studios where they were regularly employed in swing bands. Charlie Christian, a legendary young guitarist, rushed to Minton's every night from his job with Benny Goodman; trumpeter Dizzy Gillespie came over from Cab Calloway's band; and saxophonist Lester Young turned up after he finished work with Count Basie. Drummer Kenny Clarke and pianist Thelonious Monk were already on hand, for they held down steady jobs at Minton's. Saxophonist Charlie Parker, who was a wanderer, turned up often for jam sessions that soared, musically speaking, into outer space.

The musicians who put modern jazz into orbit were simply trying out musical ideas that they had been thinking about for several years. They didn't know they were creating bop. They thought of themselves, simply, as modern. As Thelonious Monk put it, "Nobody was sitting there trying to make up something new on purpose. The job at Minton's was a job we were playing. That's all."

Monk and the kindred spirits at Minton's felt that they could have the freedom of expresison they needed only within the framework of a small group. They returned to the pre-swing pattern of the jazz band in which each instrument had a single voice. They pared down the ensemble to a trumpet, saxophone, piano, drums and string bass. (Charlie Christian was an important member of the group; but after his early death, the guitar was dropped from the regular line-up.)

Bop was largely an improvised music, but it required musical training and technique far beyond the ken of the average jazzman. Dizzy Gillespie and Charlie Parker, who set the pace, were fantastic musicians. They used advanced harmonic and rhythmic ideas, weaving them around a series of chords that were the bare bones of well-known tunes. A bop number customarily began and ended with a written-down or memorized chorus played in unison. Between these two choruses, each member of the group took a solo turn.

The boppers purposely made their music too hard for run-of-the-mill musicians. Louis Armstrong, who had never been known to harbor an uncharitable thought about *any* segment of jazz, called bop "the modern malice." A few veterans of earlier jazz styles felt at home with the boppers, but most of the older musicians who flocked to Minton's to hear the new sound were confused if not downright dismayed. Almost overnight, bop made the established jazz styles sound old-fashioned.

Kenny Clarke, a member of the Minton house band, got his nickname, "Klook," short for klook-mop, because of a tricky rhythm he played on the drums.

Kenny was the first drummer of bop. He was a real revolutionary, who turned the whole theory of jazz drumming upside down. Klook had studied piano, trombone and vibes, as well as drums; and he was well schooled in music theory. For several years before he started jamming with other musical rebels at Minton's, he had been exploring new drum sounds on his own. "I was trying to make the drums more musical instead of just a dead beat," Kenny explained. "As far as I was concerned, the usual way of playing drums had become quite monotonous."

The traditional source of the steady four-four beat in jazz bands before the bop era was the bass drum. The drummer kept the foot pedal going as a matter of course and used the cymbals and snare drum for extra rhythmic effects. Kenny had the radical notion of transferring the fundamental beat from the bass drum to the top cymbal. He stopped using the foot pedal on the bass drum altogether—except for dropping an occasional "bomb"—and kept the top cymbal in motion instead.

Kenny worked the cymbal with his right hand and used

the left to improvise complicated beats on the snare. The vibration of the cymbal, which he kept in motion all through a number, produced a flowing beat. It also gave bop music a new kind of shimmering texture.

Kenny's influence has been felt all through modern jazz. He led the way for the most adventurous modern drummers, including Art Blakey and Max Roach. He now lives and works in Paris, but he is well represented on records made in this country with the Modern Jazz Quartet, Miles Davis, Dizzy Gillespie and many others.

Another member of the original Minton group was Thelonious Sphere Monk, who has been described as both "the mad Monk" and "a dour pixie." Monk is now famous, but it took years for him to win the public and critics to his spare, often dissonant, sometimes acid way of playing the piano. A man of massive integrity, Monk played as he thought right and simply waited for the listeners to catch up with him.

Thelonious was born in North Carolina in 1920 but was raised in Manhattan. He lived with his family in an apartment in a run-down neighborhood near a freight yard. When he was a teen-ager, he played piano at a nearby settlement house. Monk, who is a man of few words as well as few notes, made one of his lengthier utterances about the effect jazz has had on his life:

> Jazz is America musically. It's all jazz everywhere. When I was a kid, I felt that something had to be done about all that jazz. So I've been doing it for twenty years. . . . Jazz is my adventure. I'm after new chords, new ways of syncopating, new figurations, new runs. How to use notes differently. That's it. Just using notes differently.

When Monk was hired at Minton's, he found himself in the company of musicians who shared his exploring spirit. Some jazzmen say that he was actually the most advanced of the advanced guard.

The critics were slow to approve of Monk. Some suggested that his playing was a hoax—like the emperor's new clothes in the fairy tale. Others said that he lacked technique and couldn't play fast runs if he tried. By the mid-fifties, however, Thelonious was generally recognized as a major talent in jazz, both as a pianist and composer. Monk has written more than fifty pieces, including the beautifully melodic " 'Round About Midnight."

Monk is a big regal man whose trademarks are his goatee, dark glasses and a variety of soft hats. His glasses are prescription glasses he wears to protect his eyes against glare, and he was genuinely dismayed when legions of his fans took up dark glasses, too. He wears soft hats, including berets and various beanies, because they're easy to jam in his coat pockets. But make no mistake about it, Monk *is* a character. He speaks, eats and sleeps only when he feels like it. He often arrives late for a concert, sometimes gets up from the piano and does a little dance while the members of his group solo.

Monk composes at a grand piano in the kitchen of the apartment in which he was raised (and which he now occupies with his wife and two children). The kitchen is paneled and sound-proofed to protect the neighbors, for Monk plays for hours at a time, day or night. He constantly works to extract the *essence* of musical ideas—just as a modern abstract painter tries to extract the essence of objects in nature rather than their outward form.

Monk's music is not always stark. A good introduction to his work is "Thelonious Monk Plays Duke Ellington" (Riverside 12-201), in which Monk displays a firm swinging beat, a strong feeling for blues and an ease in lyrical passages. "Brilliant Corners" (Riverside 12-226) features Monk's own freewheeling compositions.

One of the most influential of the early boppers was guitarist Charlie Christian, a boy who was all music. Bass player
Oscar Pettiford described Charlie best. He said, "I never
heard anybody like that, who could play with so much *love*
—that's what it was, pure *love of jazz*, and great happiness
just to be part of this thing called music."

Charlie invented a new way of playing jazz guitar, just
as Kenny Clarke invented a new way of playing drums. The
mystery is how he arrived at his style, which was anything
but primitive, for Charlie had no academic training whatever.
"Where did he come from?" Teddy Hill, who was Charlie's
best friend in New York, still asks. No one knows where
Charlie got his advanced chords and complicated rhythms.
He seems to have arrived on the musical scene a full-blown
genius.

Charlie was born in 1919 in Dallas, Texas, and raised in
Oklahoma City. Oklahoma was blues territory then, and
Charlie's father was a blind blues singer and guitarist who
wandered from town to town. Charlie guided his father and
picked up some of the rudiments of guitar playing from him.

There was little schooling in Charlie's life. By the time he
was sixteen, he was working in jazz bands and touring throughout the Southwest. At nineteen he led his own small band in
a night club in Bismarck, North Dakota.

He played a Spanish type six-string guitar, which he had
had electrified. Charlie was a pioneer in using his guitar like
a horn and "blowing" long fluid solos, using a one-string,
one-note-at-a-time style. Perhaps he was inspired by the fine
tenor saxophonists who played in that section of the country
then. No one knows for sure. At any rate, Charlie arrived
early at an original guitar style that astonished other musicians.

By 1939 Charlie was working for Benny Goodman. Some
critics think Benny never sounded better than when Charlie

was feeding him riffs and rhythms and chord changes. Recordings from this period have been gathered together in "Charlie Christian with the Benny Goodman Sextet and Orchestra" (Columbia CL 652).

Charlie was well paid for the first time in his life. Everybody liked him, for he was irresistibly friendly, outgoing and generous. The only thing that Charlie needed to be completely happy was a chance to "stretch out" and play his own kind of music with a small group. When the Goodman orchestra came to New York, Charlie discovered Minton's. From the first jam session there, Minton's was his home. He hopped into a cab each night after his last set with Benny and sped uptown to the Play House.

A seat was always held for him on the bandstand. As far as manager Teddy Hill was concerned, Charlie owned the house. Teddy even bought an expensive amplifier so that Charlie wouldn't have to lug his own heavy box to the café. Minton's stayed open until 4:00 A.M., and Charlie didn't leave the stand until the last note was played. Nobody tried to cut him. Other guitarists came to Minton's, but like the pianists who listened to Art Tatum, they didn't dare compete.

Charlie loved to play with Dizzy Gillespie and Charlie Parker. No harmonic or rhythmic ideas were too difficult for him. With intuitive taste and skill, he moved into the company of the giants of modern jazz. He had only a short time to cover a long road of musical development. Charlie died of tuberculosis at the age of twenty-three.

The man who analyzed and wrote down the new musical ideas that were born at Minton's was trumpeter John Birks (Dizzy) Gillespie. Dizzy is famous for his clowning antics, but that's only the top layer of the Gillespie personality. As singer Billy Eckstine put it, "Now Diz is Dizzy like a fox, you know. He's one of the smartest guys around. Musically, he knows what he's doing backwards and forwards."

Dizzy was born in South Carolina in 1917. His father was a bricklayer and sometime musician. When Dizzy was a boy, his father played bass fiddle in a band. The other musicians stored their instruments in the Gillespie house, and Dizzy tried them all. He was also influenced by the moving song-sermons and hymns he heard at the Negro Baptist and Sanctified churches of his home town.

His father died when Dizzy was ten. By that time, the boy had shown enough musical talent to win a scholarship at an industrial training school in North Carolina. He took up trombone and trumpet at this school and studied music theory and harmony. He left school when he was seventeen, a few weeks before graduation, partly because he was having trouble with physics and partly because his mother had moved to Philadelphia. He turned up in Philadelphia with his trumpet in a paper bag.

He was a rowdy country boy and a show-off as well. But he was already so accomplished a musician that he had no trouble getting jobs in local bands. His idol in those days was trumpeter Roy Eldridge, who played with the Teddy Hill band and broadcast from the Savoy Ballroom in Harlem. When Eldridge left the Hill band, Dizzy rushed to New York and successfully tried out for his place.

Gillespie stayed with Hill for a couple of years, during which he stopped copying Eldridge and developed his own style. Kenny Clarke played drums in the same band, and together he and Dizzy worked out some advanced musical ideas. Dizzy's next job was with Cab Calloway's popular big band. He found another kindred spirit there, a brilliant young bassist named Milt Hinton.

Cab, the "hi-de-ho" king, worked at that time at the Cotton Club. Diz and Milt would go up on the roof of the club between sets and try out new harmonies. Dizzy tried to introduce these ideas in his solos. Sometimes he attempted rapid runs and high notes that he couldn't quite make. Cab would point his finger at Dizzy and say, "I don't want you playing that Chinese music in my band!"

Meantime Gillespie discovered Minton's Play House and started to jam there with Thelonious Monk and Charlie Christian. In these sessions, he improved his technique until he could handle the rapid-fire ideas that spilled out of his brain. He developed an astonishing speed and range on his trumpet.

In 1940, Dizzy met his wife Lorraine. Lorraine was dancing at the Apollo Theater in Harlem, and Dizzy, who is a talented cook, courted her by bringing her delicious meals backstage. Gillespie no longer does the cooking, but their marriage has been a happy and stable one.

Dizzy began another partnership around 1940—one that was to have deep reverberations in the world of jazz. He met and started to play with saxophonist Charlie Parker. Dizzy and Charlie jammed at Harlem after-hours spots, and for a while they played together in a big band organized by Earl Hines. The Hines band was very advanced. It was a true nursery of bop music in 1942 and 1943—unfortunately the years of a recording ban imposed by the musicians' union. The music of this band must have been phenomenal, but the group was dissolved before any records could be made.

Dizzy meanwhile continued his studies and experiments. He took lessons from a private teacher and went to symphony concerts at Lewisohn Stadium in New York. He branched out, more and more, into composing and arranging. He remembered the chord changes that he and Parker worked out at Minton's and put them all down on paper at home. By 1945, the bop revolution was in full swing. A beautiful bop classic that dates from this period is "Groovin' High" (Jazz, Vol. 11, Folkways). Listening to this number today, it's hard to imagine that bop was once called "weird" and "frantic." Dizzy and Charlie, in "Groovin' High," play light, clean, precise solos; and the parts of the composition fit together as smoothly as the parts of a watch.

From 1946 on, Dizzy usually fronted his own outfits—big bands and small combos. He was the first leader to discover that bop could be successfully blended with Afro-Cuban music. He hired a Cuban drummer, Chano Pozo, who made a sensation with the Gillespie band in 1947 at a concert at Town Hall in New York. Pozo had learned African rhythms in a secret Nigerian cult in the slums of Havana. At the concert, he crouched in the center of the stage pounding bongo drums and chanting in a West African dialect for thirty minutes. Chano Pozo was killed a few months later in a brawl in Harlem, but he left a deep impression on modern drummers.

A signal honor that came to Gillespie was that he was the first jazz musician ever sent on a good-will tour sanctioned and financed by the U. S. State Department. He made two official tours—to the Middle East and to South America— both highly successful. These tours proved that jazz is an international language that quickly dissolves differences of culture and politics. Dizzy devoted part of each show to a quick run-through of jazz history: work songs, spirituals, Dixieland, swing and modern.

Dizzy has a simple formula for getting along abroad. The first thing he does in a new country is to learn how to say "thank you" in the native tongue. He has given trumpet lessons to street urchins in Turkey and invited a snake charmer to play a duet with him in India. Wherever he goes, Gillespie's warm, generous, prankish personality wins hosts of friends for Uncle Sam.

Dizzy still wears the horn-rimmed glasses and small goatee with which he is identified around the world. He still puffs out his cheeks when he plays, an unorthodox way of blowing that makes him look like a hamster. He still uses a weird-looking horn bent upward at a 45 degree angle. (A dancer once accidentally fell against Diz's trumpet when he left it on the bandstand and bent it into that shape. Dizzy decided that he could hear himself better, and he has used an up-angled horn ever since.)

There can be no question of Gillespie's place in jazz today. One of the most respected figures in the business, he continues to be a leader in modern jazz at home and abroad. He and Charlie Parker opened a new era of experimentation and development that led to the meeting of jazz and classical music. Dizzy's only regret is that Charlie didn't live to enjoy the fruits of the jazz revolution they pioneered together.

Charlie Parker is the great tragic hero of jazz. A friend said of Charlie that he was "plugged into the main power-line of life." He was a man of bigger-than-life-size talent. He had intelligence, sensitivity and warmth. Like all musical geniuses, he seemed to have an intensity of hearing that made every waking moment a musical adventure. If he heard a dog bark or a train whistle, he translated the sounds into music. New melodies, new chords, new rhythmic ideas came tumbling out of his horn in such profusion that all jazzmen were affected by them for years afterwards.

Yet Charlie led, by any ordinary standards, a miserable life. "Hooked" on narcotics at the age of fifteen, he spent most of his life, as he said himself, "on a panic." He felt that he heard best and played best when he was off drugs, yet he was unable to reverse the self-destructive course set so early in his life.

Charlie was called "Bird." Some of his friends say that Parker got his nickname when he served a stint in the army, where recruits were called yardbirds. Others say he was called Bird because he could fly in his music as free as a bird. Birdland, the famous jazz club in New York, is named after him.

Where did Charlie Parker come from? Like Charlie Christian, he seems to have arrived full-blown on the musical scene. We know that he was born in Kansas City in 1920, took up the alto saxophone when he was eleven and was self-taught except for a little instruction in a school band. Fiercely independent from the beginning, he acknowledged no one's influence. As Bird told it himself:

> As for my beginnings, I came up in Kansas City when the joints were running full blast from nine P.M. to five A.M. . . . I was crazy about Lester [Young]. He played so clean and so beautiful. But I wasn't influenced by Lester. Our ideas ran on differently.

Parker left high school at fifteen to job around in local bands. His ideas, at that stage, were bigger than his technique. In one disastrous jam session, he tried to play "Body and Soul" in double tempo and in his own words, "everybody fell out laughing." But a few months later a guitarist at a lake resort showed Charlie the different chords and taught him to weave melodies into them. He returned to Kansas City a much better musician and got jobs in the best bands from then on. His style was more or less set while he was still in his teens. He used a smooth tone almost without vibrato and could manage flawless high-speed runs. His emotional range was wide—from a blasting church-revival style to quiet lyricism.

In 1939, Parker landed in New York broke and without a horn. Then and later, his money went to narcotics peddlers, so that no matter how much he earned he seldom had good clothes or a decent place to live. He washed dishes for a few months until he managed to get a saxophone. He went to work playing at Clark Monroe's Uptown House, a Harlem café near Minton's. Here Parker and Gillespie discovered each other. They were like two scientists working in separate laboratories who independently happen on the same theory. Bird and Dizzy discovered that they had been working along the same musical lines. They joined forces in one of the most productive partnerships of jazz history. They worked together in Earl Hines' and Billy Eckstine's bands and jammed together at the Uptown House and at Minton's.

Somewhere along the way Bird took some private lessons. He was a fast reader, a gifted composer and arranger. Other musicians accepted his talent and authority at once. Bird made his finely tuned ear the sole judge of what chords were good; and he constantly learned from classical music. He told it this way:

> First I heard Stravinsky's 'Firebird Suite.' In the vernacular of the streets, I flipped. I guess Bartok has become my favorite. I dig all the moderns. And also the classical men—Bach, Beethoven, et cetera.

Charlie didn't come to the attention of the general public until the mid-forties, when he began to record with a sextet headed by Dizzy Gillespie. This was the period that produced "Groovin' High" and many other bop works that are landmarks in the beginning of the modern jazz era. When these records were issued, Charlie was working on what was then called The Street—a row of small crowded jazz clubs along West 52nd Street in Manhattan.

A strip of this street, just west of Fifth Avenue, was the home of many bars-with-music that replaced speakeasies of the Prohibition Era. The Onyx and the Famous Door were the best known of these clubs, but the whole block rocked with a steady jazz beat. The biggest "draws" on The Street were Art Tatum, Coleman Hawkins and Billie Holiday. The jam session spirit ran high, and jazzmen carrying their horns roamed from club to club, sitting in with a half-dozen groups in a single night.

When the leaders of the bop movement arrived on The Street it became more difficult to sit in. Charlie Parker still drew hostile criticism from older musicians and some jazz writers, but he became the idol of the younger men.

Late in 1945 Bird went to Los Angeles with a group that included Gillespie and vibes player Milt Jackson. The California stay was a nightmare for Charlie. The group played for audiences that lagged musically behind those of the East and didn't "dig" bop at all. Charlie's already-frayed nervous system broke under the strain. After a chaotic recording session, he broke down completely and was committed to a state hospital for several months.

When Parker was released and came back East, he seemed completely recovered. He played with his old brilliance and made some superb recordings with his own quintet. New melodies, or ones built with fresh invention on the chords of old standards, flowed out of Charlie's mind at high speed. More and more, he reached for the outer spaces of harmony and rhythm. As he explained it, "They teach you there's a boundary line in music. But man, there's no boundary line to art."

Jazzmen, consciously or unconsciously, imitated his style on a variety of instruments. The dazzling showers of sixteenth notes that Charlie blew with such ease were copied by a whole generation of saxophonists. His unconventional rhythms and fleeting harmonies became the hallmarks of modern jazz.

Charlie made trips to France and Scandinavia when he was at the peak of his form, but the last five years of his life— between 1950 and 1955—were beset by illnesses and emotional storms. The blow that finished Parker, his biographers agree, was the death of a small daughter who had been born during his fourth marriage. Charlie's love for children was profound. When his own little girl died of pneumonia in 1954, he seemed to slide without resistance into a final spiral of self-destruction. He died of a combination of ailments in 1955.

A few days after Parker's death, there were signs scrawled on the walls of New York subways, "BIRD LIVES!" A story circulated about a tame bird that visited a musicians' bar. It was reported that a single feather floated down from the ceiling of Carnegie Hall during a jazz concert. Needless to say, this is the stuff of fables—not to be taken literally but as the expression of grief and loss felt by those touched by Bird's genius.

Some of Parker's best-known compositions are "Now's The Time," "Yardbird Suite," "Relaxin' at Camarillo" and "Confirmation." Many of his recordings can be found on the Verve or Savoy labels.

CHAPTER ELEVEN

THE MODERN SCENE

Cool Jazz and After

Soon after Charlie Parker's death, the "cool" school of modern jazz emerged. Cool jazzmen veered toward the lyrical relaxed side of bop and away from the hot shouting side. A key figure in this switch from "hot" to "cool" was Lester Willis (Pres) Young, a superb tenor saxophonist. Pres was older than Charlie Parker and spent much of his life in the midst of traditional and swing jazz; but like Parker, he was a strong individualist and had to find a style strictly his own.

Lester Young was born in 1909, the son of a carnival musician who took his family with him as he toured through the South and Southwest. Lester's father was an intelligent well-educated man, who could play any musical instrument. He tried to teach his children music, too. He started Lester on drums in the family band but then switched him to saxophone, which Lester's sister and brother played, too.

Lester hated to read music and he managed to "fake" most of the time by sitting next to his sister, who was a good reader. His father discovered that Lester couldn't play a note unless he had his sister beside him. He banished the boy from the band and made him study music for six months. "Pretty soon I could cut everybody," Lester recalled. "I was teaching other people to read."

There wasn't much time for schooling in the Youngs' roaming life. Lester left school after the third or fourth grade. He was raised in the midst of Negro blues and church music, but he was mainly inspired by two white jazzmen, Frankie Trumbauer and Bix Beiderbecke, who played in a romantic lyrical style. Lester wore out several records trying to copy the sound of Trumbauer's C-melody saxophone on his own tenor horn.

Whether or not these youthful models had anything to do with it, Pres developed a light breathy tone, a lag-along beat and a flowing relaxed style of playing. The bent notes of the blues were in his playing, too; but he strayed far from the folk roots of jazz in his search for new harmonies and new purity of sound.

Lester left his father at eighteen and played for a while with Joe Oliver, whom he described as "a very nice fellow, a gay old fellow." He spent some time in Oklahoma City and met Charlie Christian. He went to Kansas City and played there with Count Basie, on and off, for several years. In the mid-thirties he began to build the reputation that made critics call him the founder of a new school of jazz thought.

Pres said he felt "like a kid at school" with Basie, because many of the men in the band at that time couldn't read music, and they rehearsed numbers over and over until everyone learned his part. Nevertheless the Basie band gave him a fine rhythmic foundation, a springboard from which he could soar in his improvised solos. "Lester Leaps In" is a jazz classic from this period. Lester never really enjoyed big-band work, but he loved Kansas City and he could blow his freewheeling best in after-hours jam sessions.

By 1940, Pres was in New York jobbing around, leading

his own combos and jamming at Minton's. He was something of a loner, a man so sensitive that he usually wore an impassive mask to disguise his feelings. Those who knew him best said that he was sincere, gentle and good-hearted. But to the outside world, Lester seemed aloof and mysterious. He often felt frustrated by the lack of communication between the jazz artist and his audience in the usual night-club setting. He said:

> . . . I sing lyrics with my horn, and I'd like to play those slow ballads . . . but the people make so much noise . . . by the time you play a chorus and a half you wish it was long over.

He also suffered from adverse criticism. Some people told him they didn't like his light airy tone and suggested that he copy the full-bodied sound of Coleman Hawkins. "The critics," in Lester's own words, "used to call me the 'honk' man." But he couldn't change his tone—even when he gave up his old saxophone, which was held together by rubber bands, and bought a new one. In time, the public came to like the Lester Young sound and young jazzmen began to imitate him.

Lester got his nickname "Pres" when he boarded with Billie Holiday and her mother in New York. Billie called him Pres, short for president, because "he was the best." Lester, in turn, invented the name "Lady Day" for Billie and "Duchess" for her mother. Pres often recorded with Billie.

Pres died in 1959. He influenced all modern sax men, including Stan Getz, Zoot Sims, Al Cohn, Paul Desmond and Lee Konitz. Konitz says that Lester had ". . . a real beautiful tenor sax sound—pure sound. . . . He is definitely the basis of everything that's happened since." Pres recorded mainly for Verve. The "Lester Young Story" and many other Young recordings can be found on that label.

Another pioneer of cool jazz is pianist Lennie Tristano. Lennie is a hard-driving perfectionist, a tireless improviser, a man who is equally at home with a Bach fugue or the blues. His approach to music is so brainy that he has been called the Einstein of jazz. Lennie seldom performs in public, but he wields a powerful influence as the leader of a school of advanced jazz thought.

Tristano was born in Chicago in 1919. His eyesight was weak from infancy, and he was totally blind by the time he was nine years old. Between the ages of nine and nineteen, he lived in a state institution in Chicago, where the brilliant and the feeble-minded were indiscriminately lumped together. It was the kind of experience that, in Lennie's words, "either made an idiot of you or a person."

Tristano showed such striking musical talent that he was allowed to study a number of instruments at the institution. He took up piano, saxophone, clarinet and cello. In his teens he led a small band and played at local saloons. Eventually he was awarded a scholarship to the American Conservatory of Music in Chicago, where he won a bachelor's degree in music within three years.

Lennie made his way in Chicago playing with jazz groups and teaching. He was a forceful and inspiring teacher. A charter member of the "Tristano School" was alto saxophonist Lee Konitz, who began studying with Lennie while he was in high school. A classmate of Lee's, Bill Russo, took lessons from Tristano, too. Bill became one of the most important arranger-composers on the jazz scene.

Tristano's first piano model was Earl Hines. But as time went on, he found himself straying far from the path of traditional jazz. He heard the music of early bop and liked it. In his own words, "Swing was hot, heavy and loud. Bebop is cool, light and soft."

Lennie moved to New York in 1946 after the bop revolution had reached its peak. Although he was influenced by the music of Dizzy Gillespie and Charles Parker, he pursued a highly individual course. He went much further than the bop musicians in fusing classical ideas with jazz. He worked for about five years around New York in various small combos.

In 1951, Tristano turned mainly to teaching, using his home in Flushing, New York, as a studio. He lives there with his wife and young children, spending hours each day composing his difficult and complicated piano pieces. Lennie's piano sessions are grueling, for he practices left- and right-hand parts separately until they become almost automatic. He's adept at counterpoint—the art of playing two separate musical lines at once. In spite of all the preparation that goes into these compositions, Tristano improvises a great deal when he performs. His recordings are masterpieces of well-practiced improvisation.

Some of Lennie's well-known disciples are, besides Konitz, tenor saxophonist Warne Marsh and guitarist Billy Bauer. Tristano has a busy schedule of practice, teaching and recording. He occasionally makes a club or concert appearance. He long ago decided that night clubs do not inspire his best work. "It's a grueling profession," Lennie says. "The world is seen as a bar after a while." A good example of Lennie as solo pianist is "The New Tristano" (Atlantic 1357).

The role of the teacher is increasingly important on the jazz scene. One key factor in the history of modern jazz is that the musicians who came out of the army after World War II and the Korean conflict could enter universities and music schools under the G. I. Bill of Rights. They enrolled at such schools as the Juilliard School of Music in New York; North Texas State College, where there is a remarkable student jazz band; and the Mills College in California, where French composer Darius Milhaud teaches.

Miles Davis, one of the central figures of modern jazz, came to New York to study at the Juilliard School. He also studied, more informally, with Charlie Parker.

Miles was born in 1926 in Illinois and raised in East St. Louis, Missouri. His father, a well-to-do dentist, bought him a trumpet for his thirteenth birthday. A trumpet player happened to be a patient of Dr. Davis' at the time. He gave Miles lessons and taught him to play without vibrato. "You're gonna get old anyway and start shaking," he told the boy.

Miles took naturally to the trumpet. By the time he was fifteen, he had a union card and was jobbing around in local bands. Dizzy Gillespie and Charlie Parker came to St. Louis with a band while Miles was in high school—an event that proved a turning point in his life. The third trumpeter with the visiting band got sick, and Miles replaced him for two weeks. Miles loved the band's music and already knew the third-trumpet part by heart.

His mother managed to keep Miles in high school until graduation, and then his father agreed to send him to New York to Juilliard. Miles arrived in New York in 1945 and spent his first week in the city—and his first month's allowance—looking for Charlie Parker. He found Bird and roomed with him for the next year. Each night he followed Charlie around the 52nd Street jazz clubs and wrote the new chords he heard, on matchbook covers. In the daytime, he practiced these chords at Juilliard. Charlie encouraged him. He told Miles, "Don't be afraid. Go ahead and play." Before long, Miles was working on The Street with Parker.

Miles kept striving for a pure serene sound. Like Lester Young, whom he admired, he liked to play slow ballads. His tone was light and relaxed, but it had intensity, too. Under the cool surface, there was an undercurrent of deep feeling that made Miles' music very affecting. Miles has always been simple and honest about his music. He says:

You don't learn to play the blues. You just play. I don't
even think about harmony. It just comes. You learn where to
put notes so they'll sound right.

He's a true improviser—that is, he creates his solo parts
fresh with each performance. Most jazzmen repeat passages
after the first improvisation, but Miles tries to create something new each time he's on the bandstand.

Miles began to win a national reputation in 1948 when he
organized and led a nine-piece group in a series of recordings.
The band included a French horn and a tuba, which gave an
unusual texture to the total sound. The group recorded for
Capitol. Critics date the "Birth of the Cool" from the release
of a record with this title (Capitol T 762).

Miles continued to head groups—usually quintets or sex-
tets—in New York and Paris during the next few years.
Along the way, he resumed an earlier partnership with a
brilliant pianist-composer named Gil Evans. Gil had done
some of the arrangements for Miles' early records. He and
Miles found that they were remarkably well tuned to each
other's musical ideas, and they decided to do an album with
a nineteen-piece orchestra. The result was "Miles Ahead"
(Columbia 1041), a recording that brought the Davis-Evans
team international fame. Miles played a fluegelhorn (which
is a relative of the trumpet) in this album.

Miles has grown steadily in achievement and renown
since. His collaboration with Evans has produced many beautiful works. The distinctive lonely lyrical sound of the Davis
horn has been heard in several important French "New
Wave" movies.

Miles is admired not only for his music, but for his sanity,
good sense and stubborn integrity. He has also become, without meaning to be, the leader of a cult. His fans copy his
speech, his mannerisms and even his clothes. It's reported that

when Davis turned up at a San Francisco jazz club in a pin-striped suit, one of his followers exclaimed, "Pin stripes are coming back!"

At about the same time that the word "cool" was coined for modern jazz in New York, the word "progressive" came into use on the West Coast. Band leader Stan Kenton, then based at Balboa Beach in California, used the term to describe his experimental style of music.

Kenton's band served as a workshop for a number of important up-and-coming jazz talents. Open-minded and enthusiastic, Stan gave his arrangers a free hand. Pete Rugolo, Bob Graettinger and Bill Russo all produced ambitious works for him that blended modern styles of jazz and classical music.

Stan has maintained a big band over long periods of time. He has always been a strong and effective spokesman for jazz. Many of the top instrumentalists around today came up in the Kenton band.

Saxophonist Gerry Mulligan is one of the best known of the Kenton alumni. Gerry, a tall redhead who plays his big baritone sax with a rocking motion, is often seen fronting his own band. He is also a talented arranger and composer. Gerry's special contribution to the art of jazz is that he invented the piano-less quartet. He created a new sound by combining trumpet, saxophone, drums and string bass. This is a commonplace line-up now, but in 1952, when Mulligan introduced it, such a grouping seemed incredible.

Gerry was born in New York City in 1927 and raised in Philadelphia. His mother and father both played the piano, and Gerry started piano lessons at an early age. He became interested in jazz when he was in the third grade and began to write songs soon after. Naturally he was considered something of a prodigy. By high school, Gerry had switched to a horn and organized a band to play around the neighborhood.

Before he was out of his teens, he was writing for a radio band in Philadelphia.

In 1947 Mulligan came to New York to work with Gene Krupa. He wrote some arrangements for Miles Davis the following year; he also won increasing attention as a performer with an attractive light clean style. In 1952, he moved to California and joined forces with other cool musicians settled there.

Los Angeles was a center of cool jazz activity in the early fifties. Several former members of the Kenton orchestra—including trumpeter Shorty Rogers, tenor saxman Art Pepper and drummer Shelly Manne—decided to put down roots there. They liked the climate, the open spaces and the slower pace of life, and they hoped for good earnings in the movie industry. They had a few discouraging months, for California was then solid Dixieland territory, but they gathered around them an impressive group of jazz talents and gradually won the public over to the "new" sound.

Shorty Rogers was the ringleader of the school. Rogers, clarinetist Jimmy Giuffre and French horn player John Graas, all studied under the G. I. Bill of Rights with Dr. Wesley La Violette in Los Angeles. Dr. La Violette, a noted composer and teacher, has had a strong influence on jazzmen, although he writes no jazz himself.

The West Coast style of restrained understated cool jazz invaded local films, radio and television, but in time it lost its separate identity and merged into the general stream of modern jazz.

Another West Coast jazz celebrity is pianist Dave Brubeck. Dave was born in California in 1920 and raised in a highly musical family. His mother, who was a pianist, started Dave at the keyboard when he was four. At thirteen, he began to play professionally with local hillbilly, Dixieland and swing bands.

Brubeck's attention turned to classical music and its relation to jazz when he studied with Darius Milhaud at Mills College. Milhaud was one of the first European composers to become interested in American jazz. He had used jazz ideas in several early compositions. Dave got a thorough grounding in modern harmonic and tonal theories with Milhaud. He also studied for a short time with modern composer Arnold Schoenberg.

After college, Brubeck formed a chamber jazz group that played around San Francisco and won favorable notice. The members of this group included—besides Dave at the piano—alto saxophonist Paul Desmond, drummer Joe Morello and bassist Eugene Wright, all exceptional musicians. Brubeck composed many of the pieces played by the quartet; he experimented with unusual tempos and used many non-jazz elements. In 1958, the State Department sent the group on a highly successful tour of Europe and Asia.

Dave is a sincere and dedicated musician with a happy outgoing personality. He is strictly an improvisation man. He says:

> What is jazz? When there is not complete freedom of the soloist, it ceases to be jazz. . . . When we play arrangements, we try to get our freedom in the middle. We start with an arranged chorus, and then it's completely free for as long as the soloist feels like playing, and then it goes out with an arrangement.

Some critics feel that Brubeck's music lacks that elusive quality called "swing." Some Brubeck pieces jog along without much excitement, but others have a delightful pace and true jazz feeling. A fine example of better Brubeck is "Time Out" (Columbia CL 1397). Paul Desmond plays a lovely relaxed saxophone solo in his own composition, "Take Five," in this album.

It's interesting to note that a short version of "Take Five" has been played often on daytime radio programs otherwise devoted to rock-and-roll. Rock-and-roll came to the fore about 1955 and drew on the stockpile of rhythm-and-blues. Rock-and-roll singers took the strong beat and simple melodies of Negro blues and gospel songs, mixed them with a dash of hillbilly music, and created a new sound that swept the country. Popular music is an offshoot of jazz. It follows, usually with considerable time lag, the styles set by jazz. Rock-and-roll fills a need for a music that can be danced to; but unlike real jazz, it soon becomes monotonous and goes out of style. Nothing sounds less appealing than last year's rock-and-roll; but a Charlie Parker piece that dates back fifteen years, or a Louis Armstrong solo that goes back thirty-five years, still sounds fresh and beautiful.

In the field of serious jazz, a reaction to the cool style inevitably set in. In the late fifties, musicians began to cast a backward glance at the folk sources of jazz. They created a style called "hard bop" or "soul" or "funky" (meaning earthy and fundamental). The leaders of this movement were not old-fashioned instinctive musicians. They were men with good musical backgrounds, well educated in modern harmony and theory. They tried to combine the vibrant sounds of older jazz styles with a modern technical approach.

Drummer Art Blakey is the spiritual leader of the hard bop movement. His search for the roots of jazz took him to Africa, where he studied the polyrhythms of tribal music. Blakey uses these complicated rhythms in a highly charged personal style.

Blakey was born in Pittsburgh in 1919 and learned to play piano in school. His father was a businessman, who, in Art's words, "hated jazz." Art entered the jazz field as a pianist at the head of his own eight-piece band. He switched to drums when the drummer of the group got sick. Later, he freelanced and played with a number of swing and bop bands. In 1955 he again formed his own group and called it the Jazz Messengers. Many exceptional jazzmen have played with the band.

Horace Silver, who is a gifted pianist composer of the hard bop school, is a graduate of the Jazz Messengers. Horace was born in Connecticut in 1928. He studied saxophone in high school and piano privately with a church organist. His first job in jazz was with a quintet headed by cool tenor saxophonist Stan Getz, but his later career brought him into contact with Blakey and the back-to-the-roots movement.

Horace names Teddy Wilson, Art Tatum and Bud Powell as major influences; but his style is all his own—a gospel call-and-response played with ferocious drive. Silver is an amiable hard-working musician, widely respected in the jazz field.

Julian (Cannonball) Adderly and his brother Nat skyrocketed to fame with their folk-rooted style of modern jazz. Cannonball is an alto saxophonist, a large affable man, who plays with a cigarette in his hand. His eating habits, which account for his bulk, also account for his nickname. School classmates who saw him wolf down vast quantities of food called him "Cannibal," and the name was slurred in time to "Cannonball."

Cannonball has the background of serious study that has become standard for jazz musicians. Born and brought up in Florida, he taught music for eight years in a Fort Lauderdale high school. He was influenced by Lester Young and he developed a smooth flowing sound. He also became adept at high-speed runs. He arrived on the New York jazz scene in 1955 and was immediately hailed as a new Charlie Parker. This burst of publicity soon turned against Cannonball. It was too hard to live up to the billing. It took him several years, during which he played with Miles Davis and George Shearing, to build a solid reputation.

Lately, Cannonball has headed his own very successful group. His brother Nat is a fine cornetist who shows the influence of both Dizzy Gillespie and Miles Davis. The Adderly brothers played together from early boyhood. Nat went to college and studied to be a sociologist, but by 1956 he was back in the jazz field, playing often with Cannonball.

The Adderly Quintet plays with a contagious beat and campmeeting spirit. Cannonball has been accused of being slick and commercial. To the general public, however, his music is a welcome relief from too frigid or too far out jazz. Cannonball feels that his style is "an orderly chronological evolution from bop."

Some jazz musicians cannot be classified. Their work falls somewhere between "cool" and "funky" extremes. Tenor sax player Sonny Rollins belongs among the sturdy individualists of modern jazz who defy pigeonholing.

Sonny Rollins is a big strong man with a rugged face and a square-cut beard. He is an extremely serious jazz musician, who went into voluntary exile at the height of his career to study and practice.

Rollins was born in New York in 1929 and studied piano as a child. He took up the saxophone in high school, started to gig around, and cut his first record when he was eighteen. Sonny now feels that he "wasn't ready." He wasn't even sure that he wanted to stay in the music field.

Then he made a series of recordings with pianist Bud Powell and trombonist J. J. Johnson, both brilliant musicians who had mastered the bop style. Rollins caught the jazz fever and began to compose. For a while, he worked with his own trio of sax, bass and drums. By the mid-fifties, Sonny had won considerable recognition and esteem among his fellow jazzmen. His style was forceful, driving and sometimes deliberately harsh; but he showed great harmonic imagination and an unusual sense of structure in his improvised solos. Rollins could be almost sarcastic in his music. At times, he seemed to defy the audience to find any beauty in the sound of his horn.

In 1959 Sonny went into retirement. He was dissatisfied with his playing—as he said, "filled with question marks." For two years he studied piano, harmony and counterpoint with a private teacher. He gave up smoking to improve his lung power, went on a health diet and took up weight-lifting. It was difficult for him to practice on his saxophone at home without bothering the neighbors. Sonny discovered an ideal practice spot on the Williamsburg Bridge, near his home in lower Manhattan. "It's serene there," Rollins explains. "I could hear myself better. . . . You can blow as loud as you want. . . . You're up over the whole world. The grandeur gives you perspective."

Rollins returned to the jazz clubs in 1961 with a trio that included drums and guitar. He was warmly welcomed back into the front ranks of modern jazzmen.

Another man who can't be classified is bassist-pianist-composer Charles Mingus. Charlie is a well-trained versatile musician who may well hold the key to the next major development in jazz. He's an advanced experimenter, capable of using the clashing harmonies and split tones of far-out classical music. But Charlie is a "shouter" too, a man tuned to the vibrations of the basic jazz beat.

Mingus was born in Nogales, Arizona, in 1922. The family moved to Los Angeles, where Charlie went to school and studied a variety of instruments. He settled on string bass when he was sixteen and soon became so proficient that he played in many local jazz groups. Charlie's jobs eventually took him on a complete tour of jazz history. He has worked through the years with Kid Ory, Louis Armstrong, Red

Norvo, Lionel Hampton, Duke Ellington, Charlie Parker and many others.

Charlie arrived on the East Coast in the early fifties. He became known as a talented bassist with a fine large beat and blues-based intensity. But Mingus was interested in composing. Like Charlie Parker, he wanted to extend jazz beyond the boundary lines set up by previous generations. He started a long course of study with a classical bassist and addressed himself to the problem of creating a new sound within the framework of true jazz.

Mingus has been remarkably successful in his quest. His music is increasingly recognized as one of the best blends of old and new ideas around. The road hasn't always been easy. Charlie once gave up music and took a job at the post office, but as he tells it, "This security was taken away from me by Charlie Parker, who called me up, reminded me of my aesthetic responsibilities, and made me give up my chance of a pension and Blue Cross. I joined his group and took the roller coaster life of the jazzman."

Charlie Mingus is a big bearded man for whom jazz is a serious and dignified art form. His bandstand manner is usually affable and he keeps up an affectionate running banter with the young players in his group. "Work, work!" Charlie shouts at them when they get into a good groove. But Mingus can't stand phony or rude audiences. He has been known to deliver severe lectures to rowdy night-club patrons. As Robert George Reisner says in *The Jazz Titans*, "Mingus has tough fingers and a tough uncompromising nature. Like the Bird, no one messes with the man or his music."

The biggest storm of recent jazz history swirls around the head of a slight, soft-voiced, composed young man named Ornette Coleman. Ornette is a saxophonist who is clearly reaching for a sound never yet heard. He plays a plastic sax, breaks every rule in the book, and calmly explains, "I play pure emotion."

Ornette doesn't improvise on a series of chords as the bop musicians did. He improvises with the greatest possible freedom on musical "ideas"—a few notes, a rhythmic phrase or a hint of a melodic line. His approach to music is thoroughly unconventional. No figure in jazz has provoked so much controversy since Charlie Parker appeared on the New York scene.

Ornette was born in Fort Worth, Texas, in 1930. His father died when the boy was seven, and the family went on relief. They were bitterly poor, but Ornette's mother managed to scrape together enough money to buy him a cheap saxophone for his fifteenth birthday. Ornette took the sax apart and put it together again before he tried to play it. He wanted to see how it worked.

Ornette was largely self-taught. A cousin who was a music teacher influenced him. So did the music of the Negro church. He worked hard at the saxophone and soon found jobs with local bands. He next toured with a rhythm-and-blues group and eventually landed in Los Angeles.

Ornette's revolutionary ideas about jazz were beginning to take shape. He ran a freight elevator in a Los Angeles department store and spent all his spare time reading textbooks on music theory and harmony. Just as patiently as he once took his sax apart, he tried to take jazz apart to see how it worked.

When Ornette felt that he was on the track of a new kind of music, he presented his ideas to a record company. The company signed him up and sent him to a summer music school. He opened at a jazz club in New York City in the fall of 1959. With him was Don Cherry, a slender young man who plays a toy size "pocket trumpet." Ornette and Don blew some of the most spectacular call-and-response passages in jazz.

The critics have been divided into two warring camps since Ornette's first appearance. There have been many howls of outrage. But there have also been words of high praise from respected members of the jazz community. John Lewis, director of the Modern Jazz Quartet, says, "Coleman is doing the only really new thing in jazz since the innovations of the mid-forties of Gillespie, Parker and Monk." Gunther Schuller, a noted composer of classical and jazz music, is enthusiastic about Ornette's talent. Schuller wrote the notes for an excellent record titled "Ornette!" (Atlantic 1378).

It's impossible to foresee at this point Coleman's total impact on jazz. He steadily improves in technique and in the range of his ideas. His music is both very new and very old. He seems to be reaching far into the atonal future, but the core of his sound is the ancient field holler, the basic "cry" of jazz.

The logical outcome of all the study and experiment in the jazz field these days is the rise of a "third stream" of composers—men who write serious concert works that use both jazz and classical materials. "Third stream" is a term coined by Gunther Schuller who explains:

> I conceive of it as the result of two tributaries—one from the stream of classical music and one from the other stream, jazz—that have recently flowed out toward each other in the space between the two main streams. . . . The main differences between jazz and non-jazz are the improvisation and the naturally based intuitive inflections of jazz.

Schuller himself is one of the shining lights of the movement. Primarily a classical musician, Gunther plays the French horn, has worked for years in symphony orchestras and has written many classical pieces. But he also feels a strong pull toward jazz. He has produced, to date, six third-stream works, one of which was used for a jazz ballet.

A third-stream composer usually leaves spaces in his com. positions for improvisation. How the performer will fill these spaces is something of a problem. One of the solutions for the composer is to work closely with like-minded jazz musicians, as Gunther Schuller does with Ornette Coleman and as Gil Evans does with Miles Davis.

Gil Evans is a Canadian-born arranger-composer of increasing importance on the jazz scene. Gil is largely self-taught. He has been influenced by Duke Ellington, and like Duke, uses unconventional combinations of instruments. His pieces tend toward an airy lyricism that exactly suits Miles Davis' musical personality. Gil is adept at Spanish rhythms and has created some beautiful Spanish-tinged works for Miles.

John Lewis, unlike other third-stream composers, regularly appears as a jazz performer. He's the pianist as well as the musical director of the Modern Jazz Quartet. Lewis is a quiet scholarly man, well grounded in classical music. He has written a great number of light, clean cool works for the Modern Jazz Quartet, including the lovely "Fontessa" (Atlantic 1231). Although the sound of the quartet is gentle and dreamy, it is truly jazz based. A jazz pulse and blues feeling run through all Lewis works.

The Modern Jazz Quartet uses improvisation to a remarkable degree. Lewis estimates that two-thirds of each work is improvised during performance.

George Russell and Bill Russo, who are also eminent third-stream composers, depend less on chance inspiration. They leave few open spaces in their work but try to preserve the fresh spontaneous feeling of improvisation nevertheless.

George is a vital searching composer. He fell in love with jazz as a boy, when he heard Fate Marable on a river boat. Thelonious Monk had a decisive effect on him years later. He also names as major influences modern classical composers Stravinsky, Bartok and Ravel. George is interested in new tonal combinations, new rhythms, new ways of using old instruments.

Bill Russo is the author of a book, *Composing for the Jazz Orchestra*, the first of its kind. He is a vigorous, productive, vastly talented young man, who started his jazz career as a trombonist-arranger for Stan Kenton. In his many-faceted career, Bill has taught courses at the University of Chicago and the Manhattan School of Music, composed a prize-winning symphony that was performed by Leonard Bernstein, and written many jazz works. He recently composed a jazz opera.

Third-stream music requires serious attention from the jazz audience, but it offers great rewards. We live in an age of exciting listening adventure. There have never before been so many brilliant jazzmen to be heard or so many opportunities to hear them.

In the United States the cause of jazz has been enormously advanced by new recording techniques, by the mushroom growth of jazz concerts and festivals, and by the wider use of jazz of good quality on radio and television programs and on movie sound tracks. The flow of vibrant sound has kept pace with an increasing awareness and acceptance of jazz as a full-fledged art.

In the rest of the world, jazz has proved to be the most popular of American exports. Its sounds circle the globe, carried by the stepped-up communications and travel of modern life. Wherever jazz is heard, it speaks to people in a universal language, instantly and joyously understood. American jazzmen serve as invaluable ambassadors of good will. Like latter-day Joshuas, they blow their horns and the walls of fear and distrust that separate the peoples of our troubled world come tumbling down.

BIBLIOGRAPHY

Art of Jazz, The, edited by Martin T. Williams. Oxford University Press, New York, 1959.

Book of Jazz, The, by Leonard Feather. Horizon Press, New York, 1957.

Collector's Jazz, The, Traditional and Swing, by John S. Wilson. J. B. Lippincott, Philadelphia, 1958.

Encyclopedia of Jazz, The, by Leonard Feather. Horizon Press, New York, 1960.

Father of the Blues, by William C. Handy. Macmillan, New York, 1941.

Handbook of Jazz, A, by Barry Ulanov. Viking Press, New York, 1957.

Hear Me Talkin' To Ya, edited by Nat Shapiro and Nat Hentoff. Rinehart, New York, 1955.

History of Jazz in America, A, by Barry Ulanov. Viking Press, New York, 1952.

Jazz: Its Evolution and Essence, by André Hodeir. Grove Press, New York, 1956.

Jazz Makers, The, edited by Nat Shapiro and Nat Hentoff. Rinehart, New York, 1957.

Jazzmen, edited by Frederic Ramsey, Jr., and Charles Edward Smith. Harcourt, Brace, New York, 1939.

Jazz Titans, The, by Robert George Reisner. Doubleday, Garden City, New York, 1960.

Pictorial History of Jazz, A, by Orrin Keepnews and Bill Grauer. Crown, New York, 1955.

Satchmo, by Louis Armstrong. Prentice-Hall, New York, 1954.

Shining Trumpets, by Rudi Blesh. Knopf, New York, 1946.

Story of Jazz, The, by Marshall Stearns. Oxford University Press, New York, 1956.

INDEX

173